# THE PEAK DISTRICT

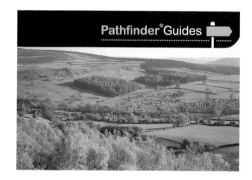

Pathfinder® Guides

## Short Walks

Compiled by
Dennis and Jan Kelsall

**Text:** Dennis and Jan Kelsall
**Photography:** Kevin Borman and Dennis Kelsall
**Editorial:** Ark Creative (UK) Ltd
**Design:** Ark Creative (UK) Ltd

© Crown copyright / Ordnance Survey Limited, 2021
Published by Trotman Publishing Ltd under licence from Ordnance Survey Limited.
Pathfinder, Ordnance Survey, OS and the OS logos are registered trademarks of Ordnance Survey Limited and are used under licence from Ordnance Survey Limited.
Text © Trotman Publishing Limited, 2021

This product includes mapping data licensed from Ordnance Survey © Crown copyright and database rights (2021) OS 150002047

ISBN: 978-0-31909-006-0

If you find an inaccuracy in either the text or maps, please contact Trotman Publishing at the address below.

First published 2001 by Jarrold Publishing. Revised and reprinted 2004, 2006, 2008.

First published 2011 by Crimson Publishing. Reprinted with amendments in 2016, 2017 and 2019.

This edition first published 2020 by Trotman Publishing. Reprinted 2021.

Trotman Publishing, 19-21D Charles Street, Bath, BA1 1HX
www.pathfinderwalks.co.uk

Printed in India by
Replika Press Pvt. Ltd. 10/21

A catalogue record for this book is available from the British Library.

**Front cover:** Mam Tor
**Previous page:** Birchen Edge

# Contents

# Keymap

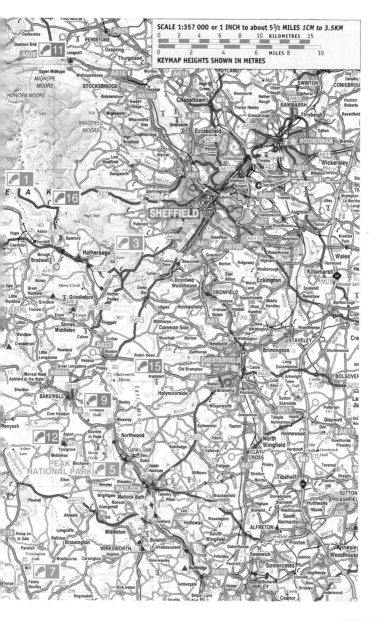

SCALE 1:357 000 or 1 INCH to about 5½ MILES *1CM to 3.5KM*

0  2  4  6  8  10  KILOMETRES  15

0  2  4  6  MILES 8  10

KEYMAP HEIGHTS SHOWN IN METRES

# At-a-glance

| 1 | 2 | 3 | 4 |
|---|---|---|---|
|  |  |  |  |
| *Fairholmes & a Sheepdog's Memorial* | *Caverns and Landslips near Castleton* | *Stanage Edge and Higger Tor* | *Dovestone Reservoir* |
| • Woodland paths<br>• huge dam<br>• Dambusters<br>• dog memorial | • Show caves<br>• limestone gorge<br>• landslipped road<br>• old mine | • Gritstone edges<br>• stunning views<br>• heather moors<br>• legendary cave | • Easy access route<br>• reservoir views<br>• gritstone scenery<br>• picnic area |
| **Walk Distance**<br>1½ miles (2.4km) | **Walk Distance**<br>2¼ miles (3.6km) | **Walk Distance**<br>3½ miles (5.6km) | **Walk Distance**<br>2¾ miles (4.4km) |
| **Time**<br>1 hour | **Time**<br>1½ hours | **Time**<br>1½ hours | **Time**<br>1½ hours |
| **Refreshments**<br>Kiosk and picnic tables at Fairholmes | **Refreshments**<br>Cafés at the caverns; pubs and cafés in Castleton | **Refreshments**<br>Seasonal ice cream van at car park; pubs and cafés in nearby Hathersage | **Refreshments**<br>Picnic tables overlooking reservoir; pubs in nearby Greenfield |
| A simple walk following clear paths and lanes, with a short climb at the start | Field paths, lanes and tracks; an energetic climb at the start | Moorland paths, occasionally rugged; dogs must be kept on a lead | Well-surfaced and graded paths |
| p. 16 | p. 20 | p. 24 | p. 28 |
| Walk Completed ☐ | Walk Completed ☐ | Walk Completed ☐ | Walk Completed ☐ |

**5**

**6**

**7**

**8**

*Robin Hood's Stride and Cratcliffe Tor*

*Gradbach and Lud's Church*

*Tissington Trail and Village*

*Wildboar- clough and Shutlingsloe*

| | | | |
|---|---|---|---|
| • Hermit's cave | • Gritstone cleft | • Picturesque views | • Dramatic summit |
| • impressive views | • woodland birds | • Tissington Hall | • expansive views |
| • striking outcrops | • former silk mill | • estate village | • wild countryside |
| • stone circle | • rock pinnacles | • limestone scenery | • flood memorial |

**Walk Distance**
3¼ miles (5.2km)
**Time**
1½ hours
**Refreshments**
Pubs in Birchover

**Walk Distance**
3 miles (4.8km)
**Time**
1½ hours
**Refreshments**
Tearoom at Gradbach Mill (weekends)

**Walk Distance**
2¾ miles (4.4km)
**Time**
1½ hours
**Refreshments**
Picnic area by car park; tearoom and pub in Tissington

**Walk Distance**
3¾ miles (6km)
**Time**
2 hours
**Refreshments**
Picnic area by car park; Crag Inn close to route

Field paths and tracks with several uphill sections; dogs must be kept on a lead

Woodland paths and tracks with steady ascents; short section of quiet lane

Fairly level tracks; gentle climb

Paths and lanes; sustained climbs

Walk Completed ☐

Walk Completed ☐

Walk Completed ☐

Walk Completed ☐

| 9 | 10 | 11 | 12 |
|---|---|---|---|
|  |  |  |  |
| *Chatsworth Park and Edensor* | *Monk's Dale and the Limestone Way* | *Langsett Reservoir* | *Youlgrave and the River Lathkill* |

| | | | |
|---|---|---|---|
| • Deer park<br>• country house<br>• pretty riverside<br>• picturesque village | • Limestone plateau<br>• old railway<br>• nature reserve<br>• resurgent river | • Heather moors<br>• ruined farm<br>• reservoir path<br>• views | • Trout streams<br>• limestone crags<br>• riverside paths<br>• high plateau |

**Walk Distance**

4 miles (6.4km) | 4¼ miles (6.8km) | 3¾ miles (6km) | 4½ miles (7.2km)

**Time**

2 hours | 2 hours | 2 hours | 2 hours

**Refreshments**

| Kiosk and picnic area at Calton Lees; tearoom at Edensor | Café by car park and pub in Miller's Dale | Café, pub and picnic area near Langsett Barn | Pubs and cafés at Youlgrave |

| Park and woodland paths and tracks; dogs must be kept on a lead on the Chatsworth estate | Field tracks and rugged woodland paths; moderate ascent; rocky paths may be slippery when wet | Good wood and moorland paths with short stretch along quiet lane; steady climb onto Hingcliff Common | Riverside and farmland paths; moderate ascent |

| p.48 | p. 53 | p. 58 | p. 62 |
|---|---|---|---|
| Walk Completed ☐ | Walk Completed ☐ | Walk Completed ☐ | Walk Completed ☐ |

| **13** | **14** | **15** | **16** |
|---|---|---|---|

| *Thor's Cave and Beeston Tor* | *Torside Reservoir* | *Monuments on the Eastern Moors* | *Ladybower Reservoir and Cutthroat Bridge* |
|---|---|---|---|
| • Impressive cave<br>• limestone scenery<br>• Manifold Way<br>• towering crags | • Pennine Way<br>• Longdendale Trail<br>• gritstone scenery<br>• high dams | • Gritstone edges<br>• great views<br>• monuments<br>• rock outcrops | • Heather moorland<br>• reservoir<br>• lovely views<br>• lost village |
| **Walk Distance**<br>3¾ miles (6km) | **Walk Distance**<br>4¼ miles (6.8km) | **Walk Distance**<br>4½ miles (7.2km) | **Walk Distance**<br>3¾ miles (6km) |
| **Time**<br>2 hours | **Time**<br>2 hours | **Time**<br>2 hours | **Time**<br>2 hours |
| **Refreshments**<br>Pub in Wetton | **Refreshments**<br>Seasonal café at visitor centre | **Refreshments**<br>Robin Hood Inn at start, pubs and tearooms at nearby Baslow | **Refreshments**<br>Ladybower Inn, picnic tables at Heatherdene |
| Farmland and riverside paths and tracks; some steep, stepped ascents | Paths and tracks; a couple of steep flights of descending steps | Moorland paths with some moderate ascents; dogs must be kept on a lead | Clear moorland paths and tracks; strenuous ascent |
| **p.66** | **p. 71** | **p. 76** | **p. 80** |
| Walk Completed ☐ | Walk Completed ☐ | Walk Completed ☐ | Walk Completed ☐ |

| 17 | 18 | 19 | 20 |
|---|---|---|---|

| *Hayfield and Lantern Pike* | *The Goyt Valley and Windgather Rocks* | *Beresford, Wolfscote and Biggin Dales* | *Kinder Scout and Jacob's Ladder* |
|---|---|---|---|
| • Rolling moorland<br>• summit viewfinder<br>• attractive village<br>• old mill | • Reservoirs<br>• heather moorland<br>• craggy outcrops<br>• woodland | • Unspoilt valleys<br>• trout stream<br>• limestone upland<br>• crags and caves | • Peat moorland<br>• fine views<br>• rock outcrops<br>• ancient routeway |
| **Walk Distance**<br>5 miles (8km)<br>**Time**<br>2½ hours<br>**Refreshments**<br>Kiosk and picnic tables at start; café at Birch Vale; pubs and cafés in Hayfield | **Walk Distance**<br>5½ miles (8.9km)<br>**Time**<br>3 hours<br>**Refreshments**<br>Picnic tables at The Street | **Walk Distance**<br>5¾ miles (9.3km)<br>**Time**<br>3 hours<br>**Refreshments**<br>Tearooms and pubs in Hartington | **Walk Distance**<br>5¾ miles (9.3km)<br>**Time**<br>3 hours<br>**Refreshments**<br>Picnic site at start; cafés and pubs at nearby Edale |
| Moorland paths and tracks; several steep ascents | Clear tracks and moorland paths; strenuous ascent | Field and riverside paths; rocky paths may be slippery when wet | Rugged moorland paths, strenuous climbs and a steep descent; *unsuitable for inexperienced walkers in poor weather*; dogs must be kept on a lead |
| p. 85 | p. 90 | p. 94 | p. 99 |
| Walk Completed ☐ | Walk Completed ☐ | Walk Completed ☐ | Walk Completed ☐ |

# Introduction

Set fairly above the heart of England where the Pennine hills dissolve into the Midland plains, the Peak District is an area of diverse and contrasting loveliness; from the expansive wildness of high peat moors to the intimate beauty of secluded limestone dales. Recognition of the area's special qualities came with its designation as the country's first National Park in 1951.

## The Two Peaks

The distinction between dark and white refers to the underlying rock of the disparate regions; rough grit and sandstone that can weather to nearly black when exposed to the elements and a light-coloured carboniferous limestone, which can appear almost white in bright sunlight. While the geological boundary between the two is abruptly distinct, the demarcation is not the simplistic division suggested by the two Ordnance Survey Explorer maps of the area.

## The Dark Peak

The Dark Peak is characterised by a rolling moorland upland, fringed in places by stark, fantastically worn cliffs and bouldery outcrops known locally as 'edges'. The hills are remarkably uniform in height, the greatest elevation of 2,088 feet (636m) being found on the Kinder. But the plateau is split by great folds and cloughs that bite deep into the heart of the central mass. During the first industrial revolution, the fast-flowing streams of these valleys were harnessed to drive textile mills, spawning villages around the periphery to accommodate the influx of workers. Later on, many of the main valleys were flooded as reservoirs to satisfy the need for water of the expanding conurbations on both sides of the Pennines. In places the stone was quarried, mainly for building, roofing and paving, but occasionally it had a quality that made it particularly useful for millstones, a fact celebrated in the National Park's adoption of a millstone as its emblem.

Many areas are important habitats for ground-nesting species of bird. Red grouse are common; indeed much of the heather moorland is specifically managed for their benefit and you can also spot birds of prey such as the hen harrier, goshawk, merlin and even peregrine falcon.

*The White Peak*
In sharp contrast, the limestone incursion is criss-crossed by lanes and peppered with farms, pretty hamlets and characterful villages. Miles of drystone walling neatly partition the countryside into fields and meadows, grazed by cattle where the grass is richest with sheep roaming elsewhere. This lower, undulating plateau is also fractured, by deep gorges, cut by torrents of glacial melt-water at the end of the last Ice Age. Such a landscape is riddled with caves, sometimes little more than a hollow.

Since the 18th-century agricultural revolution, limestone, burned in small field kilns, had been used as a fertiliser, but with the arrival of the railways, quarries were worked on an industrial scale to supply lime for building, smelting and the chemical industry

Errwood and Fernilee reservoirs from Goyt Valley

and later for the construction of roads. Quarrying still continues around Buxton, and is the main reason for its exclusion from the National Park. Mining, the other great industry of the area, no longer takes place.

The real delight of the White Peak's intrinsic charm is to be found within the confines of the valleys and dales, most too narrow for habitation or intensive farming. It is here that patches of rambling woodland are to be found, harbouring a rich variety of plants that begin a food chain supporting a population of small mammals, birds and other wildlife.

*Walking in the Peak*
The walks in this book have been devised with families in mind and are as equally suitable for newcomers to countryside walking as they are to seasoned ramblers seeking a shorter day out. Many routes include or lie close to places of interest where you can extend the day. Small museums and visitor centres interpret the area's natural and social histories, and do not forget to look around the churches, which in many ways have maintained the spirit of village life over the centuries.

Drystone wall, near Wetton

The walks are graded by length and difficulty and if you, or your children have not walked before, choose from the easier walks for your first outings. The Peak District's landscape is far from flat and even the shorter routes involve something of a climb. An indication of what to expect along the way is given under the Route Features for each walk, but the precise nature of the ground underfoot will depend upon the season and recent weather conditions; limestone can be very slippery when wet, paths can be muddy and luxuriant summer vegetation means that shorts are not recommended. Sturdy boots are the ideal footwear. Always carry waterproofs, some extra layers of clothing, an assortment of sun hats, sun cream, snacks and water.

Dogs should always be kept under control, preferably on a short lead, particularly on farmland where there is livestock and on the moors during the breeding season. In open access areas it is a requirement to keep your dog on a lead, while in some areas dogs are not allowed at all except upon public footpaths.

Remember that the countryside is a living and working environment and is constantly changing; landmarks can disappear, stiles may be replaced by gates and even rights of way are occasionally altered. However, attention to the route descriptions, reference to the maps and a little common sense will get you around without trouble. Some of the walks lend themselves to variation and consideration of the map will often suggest a shorter or longer ramble.

The times given are a guide to how long the 'average' person might take, but make no allowance for stops along the way. If you do embark upon a walk and discover that the going is harder than expected, the weather has deteriorated or you are simply taking longer than you anticipated, do not be afraid to turn back. The route will always be there for another day, when you are fitter, the children are more experienced or the weather is kinder.

This book includes a list of waypoints alongside the description of the walk, so that you can enjoy the full benefits of gps should you wish to.

For more information about route navigation, improving your map reading ability, walking with a GPS and for an introduction to basic map and compass techniques, read Pathfinder® Guide *Navigation Skills for Walkers* by outdoor writer Terry Marsh (ISBN 978-0-319-09175-3). This title is available in bookshops and online at os.uk/shop

# Fairholmes and a Sheepdog's Memorial

■ Woodland paths
■ huge dam
■ Dambuster connections
■ sheepdog memorial

*walk 1*

*This enjoyable but easy walk is an ideal starter for newcomers to countryside walking. After a gentle climb the route meanders through woodland plantation before returning beside the Derwent Reservoir. It was used during the Second World War as a practice target during training for the Dambuster raids by the RAF's 617 Squadron.*

The Derwent Dam

# *walk* 1

**START** Fairholmes
Visitor Centre

**DISTANCE** 1½ miles (2.4km)

**TIME** 1 hour

**PARKING** Fairholmes
(Pay and Display)

**ROUTE FEATURES** A simple
walk following clear
paths and lanes, with a
short climb at the start

**GPS WAYPOINTS**
  🥾 SK 172 893
  Ⓐ SK 170 892
  Ⓑ SK 169 899
  Ⓒ SK 172 895

**PUBLIC TRANSPORT**
Seasonal bus services
to Derwent

**REFRESHMENTS** Kiosk
and picnic tables at
Fairholmes

**PUBLIC TOILETS** At start

**ORDNANCE SURVEY MAPS**
Explorer OL1 (The Peak
District – Dark Peak
area)

🥾 Walk out to the lane from the visitor centre. Cross to a gate opposite the vehicle exit, where a forest path is marked as the Lockerbrook and Derwent Discovery walks. It climbs gently above a stream into mixed woodland.

---

✻ Entering the wood, look for a row of masonry piles striding across Locker Brook. They are the remnants of a **railway viaduct.** The 7-mile (11-km) track was laid up the valley in 1901 to transport stone from Bole Hill Quarry near Bamford for the construction of the Derwent and Howden dams. Once completed in 1914, the line was taken up, but temporarily opened again as far as Yorkshire Bridge in 1935 when the Ladybower Dam was being built.

---

After ¼ mile (400m), cross a bridge over a concrete water channel and immediately turn right Ⓐ towards the Derwent Dam. After another short rise, the way settles to an undulating descent. Sharp eyes will notice that some of the tree species are named. This part of the forest includes impressive western red cedars, whose needles emit a pleasant smell when crushed.

Before long, the path merges with a broad forest road. As you continue right, there are glimpses through the trees to the dam. The way ultimately drops through a gate and

The Ladybower Reservoir below Pike Low

curves at the foot of Ashton Clough to meet a lane **B**.

Cross and turn right on a raised footway beside the lane. Beyond a cattle-grid is a lakeside viewpoint where information boards describe the dam's construction, while nearby is a memorial to a faithful sheepdog. She guarded her dead master's body after he died on the bleak Howden Moors during the winter of 1953–4. Despite many searches it was 15 weeks before he was found and the stone slab was erected to honour the dog's devotion.

Tucked inside the western dam tower is a memorial to the **Dambusters** of 617 Squadron. During the Second World War, the squadron trained here in preparation for a raid on the German dams of the industrial Ruhr in order to disrupt the Nazi war machine. The valley was subsequently used during the making of the 1955 film *The Dam Busters*, starring Michael Redgrave and Richard Todd.

*What was the name of the loyal sheepdog commemorated here?*

Just beyond the dam, a stepped footpath signed to Fairholmes leaves beside a small parking area. Keep left where it forks, descending more steps to emerge onto a lane **C**.

To see the dam at close quarters, go left over a bridge spanning the outflow and then cut across an open grass area towards the foot of the steep, stone embankment. To return to the car park, retrace your steps over the bridge. Abandon the lane just a few yards beyond the point at which you first joined it along a footpath on the left. It leads back to the visitor centre. ■

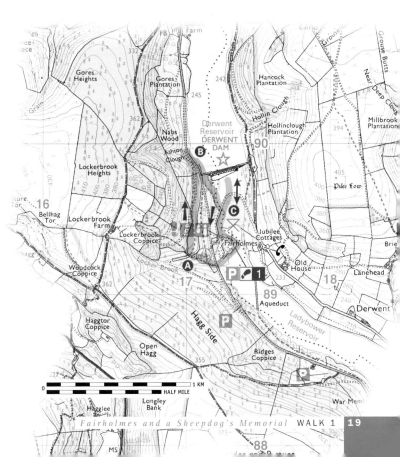

# Caverns and Landslips near Castleton

- Show caves
- limestone gorge
- landslipped road
- old mine

*Castleton is renowned for its show caves and this walk takes you past three of them; Speedwell, Treak Cliff and Blue John. After climbing from the foot of Winnats Pass across the hillside, the route follows an old road, abandoned after years of landslip, to pass a former lead mine.*

*walk 2*

The crumbling road below Mam Tor

# walk 2

**START** Winnats

**DISTANCE** 2¼ miles (3.6km)

**TIME** 1½ hours

**PARKING** Speedwell Cavern long stay car park (Pay and Display) – fork right off A6187, ¼ mile (400m) west of Castleton

**ROUTE FEATURES** Field paths, lanes and tracks; an energetic climb at the start

**GPS WAYPOINTS**
- SK 140 828
- Ⓐ SK 136 831
- Ⓑ SK 131 834
- Ⓒ SK 134 834

**PUBLIC TRANSPORT** Bus services to Castleton

**REFRESHMENTS** Cafés at the caverns; pubs and cafés in Castleton

**PUBLIC TOILETS** In Castleton and at Speedwell Cavern short stay car park

**ORDNANCE SURVEY MAPS** Explorer OL1 (The Peak District – Dark Peak area)

Leave the back of the long stay car park over either of the stiles, heading upfield to the Speedwell Cavern. Even if not visiting the cave, it is worth a brief detour into Winnats Pass, a narrow gorge flanked by dramatic limestone cliffs along which the lane tackles a 1 in 5 gradient.

Continue from the short stay car park over a pair of stiles beside the toilets, curving left around the slope to a gated stile in a wall. Contour on above the lane, eventually joining a concrete pathway to Treak Cliff Cavern Ⓐ.

Walk behind the visitor centre and carry on across the hillside, from which there is a grand view along the Hope Valley. Before long, the path turns beside a gully, climbing more steeply to a pair of gates. That on the right accesses a viewpoint looking across to Mam Tor, the 'Shivering Mountain'. However, the onward path lies through the gate ahead, which crests a rise to reach the Blue John Cavern. Follow the access drive out to a lane and turn right, walking down to a turning circle at the end.

Pass through a gate Ⓑ to pick your way along what remains of the lane, its surface contorted and ruptured by the relentless slip of the mountainside. Follow its fractured course for ½ mile (800m) down the hill, the way turning a hairpin bend at the bottom. Farther on, a gash in the hillside over to the right is the site of the Odin Mine, which can be reached through a gate. It was worked for lead, perhaps since Roman times, until it finally closed around 1870.

Immediately after the mine, look out for a gate on the left **C**, which leads to the processing area. A stone wheel lies acant

Called the **'Shivering Mountain'**, the flank of Mam Tor is undergoing a giant landslide that began some 4,000 years ago. The ground remains unstable and continues to slump down the hillside, the movement exacerbated by water seepage after prolonged periods of rainfall. The road, opened as a turnpike in 1810 became the main thoroughfare between Castleton and Chapel en le Frith. However, it needed constant repair and was finally closed in 1979.

*Look for a milepost beside the road, just before the Odin Mine, how far is it to Sheffield?*

Mam Tor and Lose Hill Ridge from Odin Mine

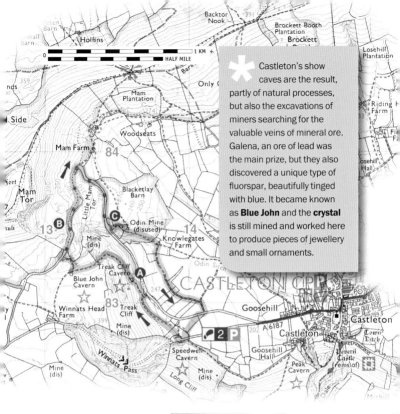

beside a circular track, where the lumps of ore were crushed prior to sorting and smelting. Beyond the crushing circle, cross a wooden bridge and carry on over stiles to Knowlegates Farm. Winnats is signed to the right along the access

The crushing circle at Odin Mine

track, which joins another track to lead back to the lane. The car park is then just to the right.

# Stanage Edge and Higger Tor

- Gritstone edges
- stunning views
- heather moors
- legendary cave

*Heather and gritstone moors are a distinct feature of the Dark Peak and this undemanding walk evokes the sense of their wild and rugged character. The route follows a dramatic gritstone edge, which is a popular haunt for rock climbers.*

walk 3

The trig pillar at the southern end of Stanage Edge

# walk 3

**START** Upper Burbage Bridge

**DISTANCE** 3½ miles (5.6km)

**TIME** 1½ hours

**PARKING** Upper Burbage Bridge car park

**ROUTE FEATURES** Moorland paths, occasionally rugged; dogs must be kept on a lead

**GPS WAYPOINTS**
🖉 SK 260 830
Ⓐ SK 254 830
Ⓑ SK 250 830
Ⓒ SK 244 835
Ⓓ SK 253 825
Ⓔ SK 257 821

**PUBLIC TRANSPORT** Seasonal bus service

**REFRESHMENTS** Seasonal ice cream van at car park; pubs and cafés in nearby Hathersage

**PUBLIC TOILETS** None

**ORDNANCE SURVEY MAPS** Explorer OL1 (The Peak District – Dark Peak area)

🖉 Leaving the car park, follow the lane left to a sharp bend. Keep ahead past a large boulder along a path striking across the moor towards distant crags. After some 550 yards, look for a memorial tablet set among the stones of the path Ⓐ.

> ❓ *Who is commemorated on the memorial stone?*

To the right, a heathery trod leads to the Cowper Stone, a massive detached outcrop, which is a favourite challenge for rock climbers.

Return to the main path and carry on towards the crags. Soon the route steepens as it clambers briefly between rocks onto the southern end of Stanage Edge. Levelling off, the way bears left and, becoming flagged, leads to a triangulation pillar perched prominently upon the highest of the massive gritstone boulders littering the top.

After savouring the view, continue north-west for some 40 yards to find a path dropping left from the scarp through a notch in the rocks Ⓑ. Take note of the spot, for it marks the way off the ridge on the return leg.

For the present, however, keep ahead along the escarpment, *being careful not to stray too*

Looking west from Stanage Edge

At one time these moors formed part of the Duke of Rutland's grouse shoot and public access was forbidden. But the prohibitions did not deter everyone and climbers from Sheffield used **Robin Hood's Cave** as a 'bivvy' or overnight shelter during surreptitious weekend climbing expeditions.

*close to the edge in enjoying the superb vistas.* The trail weaves between the boulders, which in places have been eroded into remarkable shapes. The airy walk offers fine views across the valley to Eyam and Offerton moors as well as the more distant profiles of Win Hill, Lose Hill, Mam Tor and Kinder Scout.

After ½ mile (800m), look out for a stony path leaving half-left **C**. It descends briefly through a cleft in the rock to a small shelf, behind which natural erosion has scooped cubbyholes from the soft rock. You can clamber through the main one to a 'window' that frames an expansive scene. This is Robin Hood's Cave, one of many local natural features having supposed connections to the legendary hero.

Stanage Edge from Higger Tor

Retrace your outward steps along the scarp. Approaching the triangulation pillar, take the descending path to the right seen earlier **B**. It drops below a small quarry from which millstones were cut. Several still lie nearby, abandoned after the quarry closed.

Continue across the moor to a fork. Keep left above the lane, dropping to it a little farther on **D**. Go over the stile opposite and bear half-left to meet another lane. Again cross and follow a stepped path onto Higger Tor, walking on to the top of the summit.

The heathery plateau extends to the right offering a magnificent panorama across the upper Burbage Valley. Some ¼ mile (400m) to the south is the lower promontory of **Carl Wark**, defended by a high wall of massive boulders. Although commonly regarded as a fort, its true purpose is not really known and it may date from the Iron or possibly even the Bronze Age.

Return to the top of the steps where you arrived on Higger Tor **E**, to find a small wooden waymark indicating a path north. It undulates easily along the side of the valley, presently returning you to the car park. ■

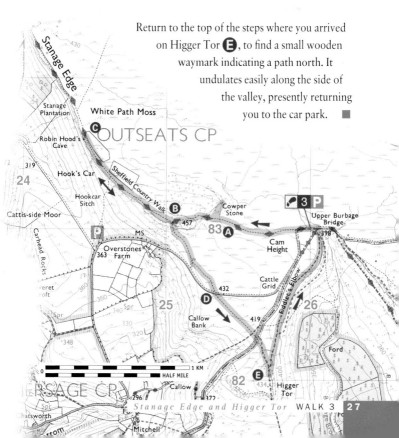

# Dovestone Reservoir

■ Easy access route   ■ wild gritstone scenery
■ reservoir views      ■ picnic area

*walk 4*

*An easy route and impressive scenery come together on this circuit of the Dovestone Reservoir (also often spelt Dove Stone), the lowest and largest in a chain of three artificial lakes crowded into the narrow, upper valley of Greenfield Brook. As the path is surfaced for buggies and wheelchairs, it makes for a relaxing stroll.*

*Alderman's Hill and Dovestone Reservoir*

# walk 4

**START** Dovestone
Reservoir

**DISTANCE** 2¾ miles (4.4km)

**TIME** 1½ hours

**PARKING** Dovestone
Reservoir car park (Pay
and Display)

**ROUTE FEATURES** Well-
surfaced and graded
paths

**GPS WAYPOINTS**
🥾 SE 013 033
Ⓐ SE 019 031
Ⓑ SE 019 038
Ⓒ SE 022 042
Ⓓ SE 020 045

**PUBLIC TRANSPORT** Bus
services to nearby
Greenfield

**REFRESHMENTS** Picnic
tables overlooking
reservoir; pubs in nearby
Greenfield

**PUBLIC TOILETS** At start

**ORDNANCE SURVEY MAPS**
Explorer OL1 (The Peak
District – Dark Peak
area)

🥾 Leaving the far end of the car park, follow the ongoing lakeside track past the Dovestone Sailing Club and jetty. Through a gate, the track continues beside a yacht storage compound, shortly reaching a bridge across the foot of Chew Brook.

At the junction immediately beyond Ⓐ, bear left. Over a second bridge, the path rises beside a memorial plantation, the increasing height opening a wonderful panorama to Alderman's Hill.

> ✳ **Alderman's Hill** is named after a **giant** who fell out with his neighbour Alphin over the affections of Rimmon, the beautiful water nymph of Chew Brook. They began hurling the boulders, which now scatter the hillside, and Alderman slew his opponent with a lucky shot. But Rimmon favoured Alphin and, devastated by his death, flung herself off the cliffs. She lies buried with her lover on the flanks of Alphin Pike.

Through a gate beside a single silver birch, the way carries on above the water. The eye is drawn to the upper reaches of the valley while the craggy outcrop of the Great Dove Stone rears high above.

After ¼ mile (400m), at the corner of a larch plantation, *a gate on the left* Ⓑ *offers the option of descending the grassy slope to*

*Dovestone Reservoir and Great Dove Stone Rocks*

continue beside the lakeshore. However, the easy access route lies ahead, shortly passing through a gate to a picnic area before crossing a stream below Ashway Gap **ⓒ**. *The optional route rejoins the main track to cross the bridge.*

Climbing gently beyond, the path then swings across the Yeoman Hey Dam to a junction on the other side of the valley.

You can extend the walk by following the service track right for 1½ miles (2.4km) to the head of the main valley. The scenery becomes increasingly wild, particularly during the winter months, when blankets of snow can overhang the upper crags.

The return, however, lies along the track to the left. After some 30 yards, leave left through a gate **ⓓ**, from which a path falls beside woodland plantation towards the lake. Running level at the foot of Alderman's Hill, the way affords a superb view across the water into the side valley of Chew Brook. A reservoir, unseen at its head, is one of the highest in England.

> **?** *Whose visit is commemorated by a plaque set at the western end of the Yeoman Hey Dam?*

> **✳** The picnic area stands on the site of a 19th-century hunting lodge, **Ashway Gap House**. After the construction of the reservoirs, it was occasionally used for board meetings by the Waterworks Committee and during both World Wars was requisitioned as a hospital. It was finally demolished in 1981.

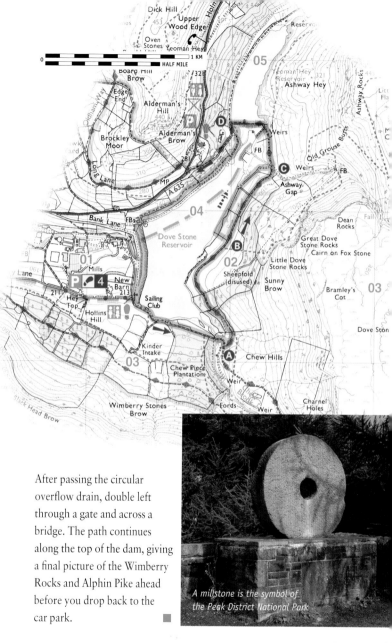

After passing the circular overflow drain, double left through a gate and across a bridge. The path continues along the top of the dam, giving a final picture of the Wimberry Rocks and Alphin Pike ahead before you drop back to the car park.

*A millstone is the symbol of the Peak District National Park*

# Robin Hood's Stride and Cratcliffe Tor

- ◼ Hermit's cave
- ◼ impressive views
- ◼ striking rock outcrops
- ◼ prehistoric stone circle

*walk 5*

*The gritstone outcrops surrounding Birchover are full of interest, as revealed in this enjoyable ramble from the village. A hermit's cell, ancient stone circle and intriguing rooms carved behind rocky terraces are just some of the curiosities encountered along the way.*

*From Cratcliffe Tor to Robin Hood's Stride*

**START** Birchover

**DISTANCE** 3$\frac{1}{4}$ miles (5.2km)

**TIME** 1$\frac{1}{2}$ hours

**PARKING** Considerate street parking in village

**ROUTE FEATURES** Field paths and tracks with several uphill sections; dogs must be kept on a lead

**GPS WAYPOINTS**
SK 236 621
Ⓐ SK 233 619
Ⓑ SK 228 615
Ⓒ SK 228 618
Ⓓ SE 225 623

**PUBLIC TRANSPORT** Bus service to Birchover

**REFRESHMENTS** Pubs in Birchover

**PUBLIC TOILETS** In Birchover

**ORDNANCE SURVEY MAPS** Explorer OL24 (The Peak District – White Peak area)

Take the narrow, descending lane leaving on the bend beside the inn at the lower end of the village. Walk past the church and the Old Vicarage with its ornamental pond, leaving just beyond along a footpath on the left. It rises to regain the track, where you should go left to Rocking Stone Farm.

*What is the unusual name of the inn passed at the start of the walk?*

Reaching a sharp curve Ⓐ, go through a stile beside a gate and turn right by the wall. The path passes the ruin of a barn and then loses height by a stand of Scots pine to meet a green track. Follow it left, passing through a squeeze stile beside a little barn and continue down the field edge. Over stepping stones at the bottom, climb out to the B5056.

Cross to a footpath opposite and head up a small field to emerge beside a stone cottage onto Dudwood Lane Ⓑ. Walk down to a bend and keep ahead along a drive, signed the Limestone Way Ⓒ. After passing through a stone gateway, leave the track, bearing half-left on a grass trod. Go through a gate near Hilary's seat and follow the ongoing track to the top Ⓓ.

Weasel Pinnacle at Robin Hood's Stride

It would take long legs to step between the two pinnacles of **Robin Hood's Stride**, for they are 50 feet (15m) apart. Known as 'Weasel' and 'Inaccessible', they provide a challenge for rock climbers. The outcrop is alternatively known as 'Mock Beggars' Hall' because of its silhouette when seen from afar.

Through the gate ahead, you can see across the fields to Nine Stones Circle. Only four of the stones still stand, the tallest in Derbyshire and known as the Grey Ladies, they supposedly come to life and dance at midnight. Robin Hood's Stride is the striking outcrop of rock over to the left, accessed over a stile. Children will enjoy scrambling over the rocks, but *watch they do not get into difficulty.*

Cratcliffe Tor lies to the east, hidden behind trees. To reach that, go back to the top of the track and head down right 50 yards to find another stile on the left. Walk away at the edge of the trees over a rise, and bear right to a stile hidden in the corner. There is a grand view from the top, *but be careful for the eastern edge is a sheer drop.* To find the Hermit's Cave, walk ahead from the stile around the base of the rocks.

The interconnecting rooms and seats of the **Rowtor Rocks**, were cut from the natural stone outcrop by the Reverend Thomas Eyre, a 17th-century vicar of the church. He brought his friends up here to enjoy the thrilling view across the valley.

The entrance is hidden by a couple of yews. The cave is protected behind a railing, but inside, you can see a crucifix carved on the rear wall.

Return to the track and retrace your steps to the corner of Dudwood Lane **C**. Walk out to the main road and go left for 150 yards, crossing to a gate on the right. A path slants steeply upfield, emerging over another stile onto the track you followed earlier.

The Hermit's Cave

Now, however, turn left around the wooded base of the hilltop. Meeting the bend of a track, take the left fork, picking up your outward path past the old vicarage and church back to the village. To visit the Rowtor Rocks, just before reaching the inn, take a path off to the left, which climbs to the outcrop. The return is by the same path. ■

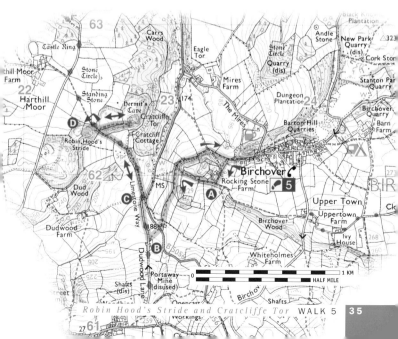

# Gradbach and Lud's Church

- ■ Gritstone cleft
- ■ woodland birds
- ■ former silk mill
- ■ rock pinnacles

*The River Dane runs a short but pretty course through the western Peak District to the Cheshire Plain, here flowing through a deep, wooded ravine. Striking rock features and a mysterious chasm are also visited before winding back through the trees above a babbling stream.*

*walk 6*

Back Forest

# walk 6

**START** Gradbach

**DISTANCE** 3 miles (4.8km)

**TIME** 1½ hours

**PARKING** Car park off minor lane, ½ mile (800m) east of Gradbach Youth Hostel

**ROUTE FEATURES** Woodland paths and tracks with steady ascents; short section of quiet lane

**GPS WAYPOINTS**
- ✒ SJ 998 662
- Ⓐ SJ 990 657
- Ⓑ SJ 985 657
- Ⓒ SJ 986 657
- Ⓓ SJ 995 649
- Ⓔ SJ 990 656

**PUBLIC TRANSPORT** None

**REFRESHMENTS** Tearoom at Gradbach Mill (weekends)

**PUBLIC TOILETS** None

**ORDNANCE SURVEY MAPS** Explorer OL24 (The Peak District – White Peak area)

✒ Leaving the car park, follow the lane right, branching after 200 yards along a drive on the right. The drive leads to Gradbach

> **? What are the initials on the gatepost and what do they stand for?**

Mill, built to produce silk in the 18th century. Wind in front of the main building and then go left along a short riverside path. Rising to a gate, continue briefly at the field edge before slipping over a stile onto an adjacent track. Where it subsequently bends sharply left, leave ahead over a stile to find a footbridge spanning Black Brook Ⓐ.

A sign directs you ahead towards Danebridge and Swythamley. Climb past a second sign in the direction of Swythamley to meet a crossing path and go right. The onward way rises through Forest Wood.

The path eventually levels and reaches a signpost Ⓑ beside a small clearing, where two outcrops of rock to the right stand proud above the valley. Their platforms provide great viewpoints and youngsters will enjoy exploring the crevices, but *take care that they do not fall.*

Back at the signpost, the way to Lud's Church is indicated to the left, doubling back above the path on which you arrived. After 200 yards, look for a turning off on the right **C** and go through a crack in the sandstone cliff. A

> ✳ Local tradition holds that the secluded hideaway of Lud's Church was a meeting place for Lollards, followers of the 14th-century religious reformer John Wycliff. Challenging the practices of the established Church, his doctrines were viewed as heresy. It is supposedly named after one of the group's members, Walter de Ludank. The chasm is also said to be the **Green Chapel**, in which King Arthur's knight, Sir Gawain slew the Green Giant.

steep flight of rock-cut steps descends into the gloomy canyon of Lud's Church, whose walls are draped with dripping ferns and moss.

Wander through, choosing the right branch towards the far end to climb out up a stepped path. Carry on between the trees, later passing a path off on the right before reaching a T-junction. Turn right towards Roach End, eventually reaching a second junction among beech trees, from which a path is signed sharp left to Gradbach **D**.

After an initial steep drop, the gradient eases. Remain on the higher path at a fork, only later closing with Black Brook to reach a ford **E**. There is neither footbridge nor stepping stones, but if the water is low it can be crossed with no great difficulty to a rising track on the opposite bank.

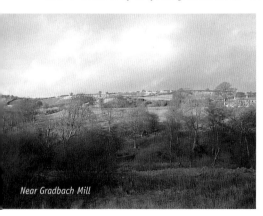

*Near Gradbach Mill*

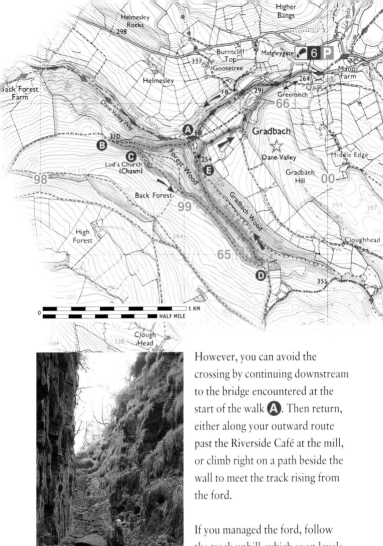

However, you can avoid the
crossing by continuing downstream
to the bridge encountered at the
start of the walk **A**. Then return,
either along your outward route
past the Riverside Café at the mill,
or climb right on a path beside the
wall to meet the track rising from
the ford.

The moss-hung cleft of
Lud's Church

If you managed the ford, follow
the track uphill, which soon levels
as it leaves the trees. Keep ahead as
other tracks join, the way becoming
metalled and ultimately taking you
back to the car park.

# Tissington Trail and Village

- ■ Picturesque views
- ■ Tissington Hall
- ■ attractive estate village
- ■ limestone scenery

*Following part of a former railway line, now adopted as the Tissington Trail, this undemanding ramble explores the countryside around one of the Peak District's many pretty villages. There are fine views over the neighbouring valley to Parwich and youngsters can enjoy finding the village wells, which are dressed in flowers each spring.*

*walk 7*

Tissington Hall

# walk 7

**START** Tissington

**DISTANCE** $2\frac{3}{4}$ miles (4.4km)

**TIME** $1\frac{1}{2}$ hours

**PARKING** Tissington
Trail car park (Pay and
Display)

**ROUTE FEATURES** Fairly
level tracks; gentle climb

**GPS WAYPOINTS**
SK 178 520
Ⓐ SK 171 537
Ⓑ SK 172 526

**PUBLIC TRANSPORT**
Bus service to nearby
Tissington Gate

**REFRESHMENTS** Picnic
area by car park;
tearoom and pub in
Tissington

**PUBLIC TOILETS** At start

**ORDNANCE SURVEY MAPS**
Explorer OL24 (Peak
District – White Peak
area)

From the car park, begin along the Tissington Trail, heading north-east beneath a bridge. Running within a tree-lined cutting, it soon curves left, later passing beneath a second bridge. Beyond, the views open out past Shaw's Farm across the valley of Bletch Brook.

Opened in 1899, the LNWR line between Ashbourne and Buxton was in service for only 68 years. In a pioneering project to reopen such routes as leisure trails, the Peak Planning Board later purchased the line and **the Tissington Trail** was eventually inaugurated in 1971. An immediate success, enjoyed by countless cyclists and walkers it has provided a model for similar schemes across the country.

The trail, pleasantly lined with hawthorn, ash and bramble, shortly delves into another short cutting and beneath a third bridge. Keep going for a further 300 yards to find a crossing path marked by a signpost Ⓐ.

Over a stile on the left, the way is signed to Tissington. The path strikes half-right across the field to the corner, continuing along a section of walled track. The track runs on at the edge of successive fields, which, farther on, are rumpled in long lines of ridge and furrow.

*The track back across the fields*

Eventually, the way culminates along a short stretch of rough, walled track to meet the corner of Rakes Lane **B**. Follow the street down into the village, passing Tissington Hall, set back on the right and then the church on the left. Go left at the end and then keep right, soon returning to the car park entrance.

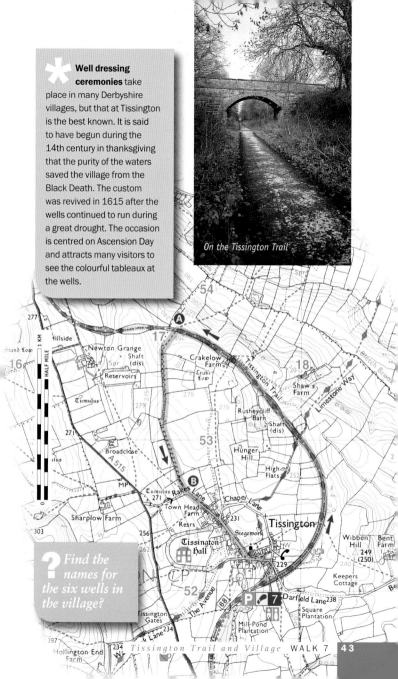

**Well dressing ceremonies** take place in many Derbyshire villages, but that at Tissington is the best known. It is said to have begun during the 14th century in thanksgiving that the purity of the waters saved the village from the Black Death. The custom was revived in 1615 after the wells continued to run during a great drought. The occasion is centred on Ascension Day and attracts many visitors to see the colourful tableaux at the wells.

*On the Tissington Trail*

? Find the names for the six wells in the village?

# Wildboarclough and Shutlingsloe

- Dramatic summit
- wild countryside
- expansive views
- flood memorial

*walk 8*

*Wildboarclough lies in a secluded, sheltered valley below the steep slopes of Shutlingsloe, which, although of only modest height, has a dramatic profile that has earned it the title of the 'Cheshire Matterhorn'. This walk takes a roundabout route to the top, returning past the scattered dwellings of Wildboarclough for a final view of the peak from the other side of the valley.*

*Looking east from Shutlingsloe summit*

# walk 8

**START** Clough House

**DISTANCE** 3¾ miles (6km)

**TIME** 2 hours

**PARKING** Clough House car park

**ROUTE FEATURES** Paths and lanes; sustained climbs

**GPS WAYPOINTS**

✏ SJ 987 698
Ⓐ SJ 986 697
Ⓑ SJ 982 690
Ⓒ SJ 979 694
Ⓓ SJ 975 699
Ⓔ SJ 982 686
Ⓕ SJ 988 687

**PUBLIC TRANSPORT** None

**REFRESHMENTS** Picnic area by car park; Crag Inn close to route

**PUBLIC TOILETS** None

**ORDNANCE SURVEY MAPS** Explorer OL24 (The Peak District – White Peak area)

✏ Exit the car park by the entrance nearest to Clough House Farm. Cross a bridge and pass the buildings, then turn right into the yard. Leave through a waymarked gate at the end on the left and swing right, heading downfield to a footbridge Ⓐ.

Cross the lane to a track, which is signed to Langley via Shutlingsloe and rises gently to the left. Over a stile, carry on beside a pine plantation to a cottage, Banktop. Walk along its access to a junction by a cattle-grid Ⓑ.

Go sharp right, following a rising track across open grazing. Abandon it just before a gateway, ascending left and crossing a stile. Keep heading uphill to a second stile, passing onto the rougher hill pasture Ⓒ.

Strike half-right and then, a few yards farther on, bear right again, contouring the hillside above a wall. Eventually passing through a gate, turn half-left to climb through a shallow valley of eroded shale. Emerging at the top, the ground levels. Ignoring a crossing path, keep ahead, avoiding the bog of a hollow on a straddling plank. The path leads to a gate at the end of a wall Ⓓ.

Instead of passing through, follow a flagged path left towards Shutlingsloe. Over a stile the going steepens in a final strenuous pull to the summit. The panorama is superb in every direction and near the triangulation pillar is a topograph that helps identify some of the surrounding hills.

Just beyond the pillar, look for a waymark indicating the downward path to the left. Those with short legs may find the first section a bit of a scramble, but the gradient soon eases as the descent runs onto the grass below. Picking up your outward route, walk back down to the cattle-grid at **B**.

This time, stay ahead on the main track, following it down to meet a lane **E**. A short distance to the right, you will find the Crag Inn, but the way back lies to the left. Reaching a junction, turn off right over a bridge spanning Clough Brook, where a memorial plaque records the Wildboarclough flood, which destroyed the original structure and drowned a man in his car.

**?** *On what date did the flood disaster of Wildboarclough occur?*

Head up the quiet lane, passing an impressive private house set back on the left. It was originally the offices for a carpet mill, which has long been demolished, and more

*Shutlingsloe from above Wildboarclough*

recently claimed the honour of being the largest sub-post office in England.

At the top of the hill ⑰, go left towards Macclesfield Forest. The way levels to give a grand view across the valley to Shutlingsloe before descending back to Clough House and the car park.

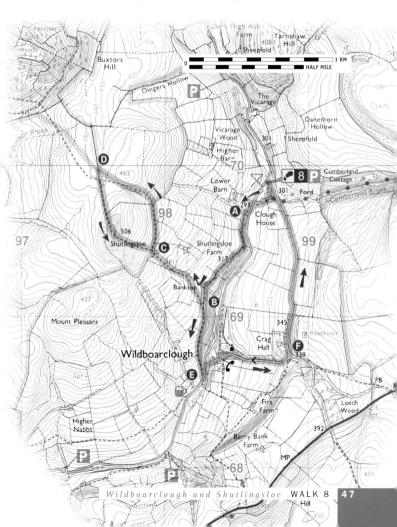

# Chatsworth Park and Edensor

- Deer park
- country house
- pretty riverside
- picturesque village

*walk 9*

*Chatsworth is arguably the most famous stately home in the country and is seen in all its grandeur during this leisurely ramble across the rolling estate. Among the other highlights is the charming estate village of Edensor and perhaps a sight of the herd of fallow deer that roam the park.*

*Looking south along the River Derwent*

# walk 9

**START** Calton Lees

**DISTANCE** 4 miles (6.4km)

**TIME** 2 hours

**PARKING** Calton Lees car park (Pay and Display)

**ROUTE FEATURES** Park and woodland paths and tracks; dogs must be kept on a lead on the Chatsworth estate

**GPS WAYPOINTS**
- SK 258 685
- **A** SK 257 701
- **B** SK 249 698
- **C** SK 246 689
- **D** SK 244 685

**PUBLIC TRANSPORT** Bus service to Chatsworth

**REFRESHMENTS** Kiosk and picnic area at Calton Lees; tearoom at Edensor

**PUBLIC TOILETS** None

**ORDNANCE SURVEY MAPS** Explorer OL24 (The Peak District – White Peak area)

Leaving the Calton Lees car park, take a surfaced path back to the main road, crossing near a white gateway and cattle-grid. Head down the grassy slope past the ruin of a corn mill and turn left to follow the River Derwent upstream. Carry on past two impressive weirs, eventually reaching a bridge carrying the main drive to the house **A**.

Chatsworth House lies across the river, its formal gardens elevated on a terrace and presenting an imposing façade to approaching visitors. Wander over the bridge and bear

> William Cavendish, the first Duke of Devonshire, built Chatsworth House on a scale befitting his position as head of one of the country's leading families and it became known as the '**Palace of the Peak**'. The work took more than 20 years and was completed in 1707. The internal decoration is equally lavish and a tour of the house includes the state rooms, baroque chapel, painted hall, oak room (with superb wood carvings) and magnificent library. A new north wing, added in the early 19th century, included an orangery, dining room, music gallery and sculpture gallery.

left to see Queen Mary's Bower, where Mary Queen of Scots was reputedly allowed to take exercise during her imprisonment at Chatsworth under the sixth Earl of Shrewsbury. The house and gardens are open

Joseph Paxton, who also created the famous Emperor Fountain to honour a visit by the Tsar of Russia, which never materialised, extended **Chatsworth's formal gardens**. The extensive park is the work of 'Capability' Brown who set out the random groups of trees and even straightened the river. The removal of Edensor to its present site completed the process, for neither man nor Nature was allowed to stand in the way of the grand design.

throughout the year and, if you have time, well worth a visit.

Go back across the bridge, forking right off the main drive just beyond in favour of a path rising over the shoulder of a grassy hill. It drops to the road opposite the entrance to Edensor, which is pronounced 'Ensor'. Carefully cross and follow the lane into the village. If looking for refreshment, bear left of the church to find the post office where there is a tearoom, otherwise pass right of the church along the main street.

Queen Mary's Bower

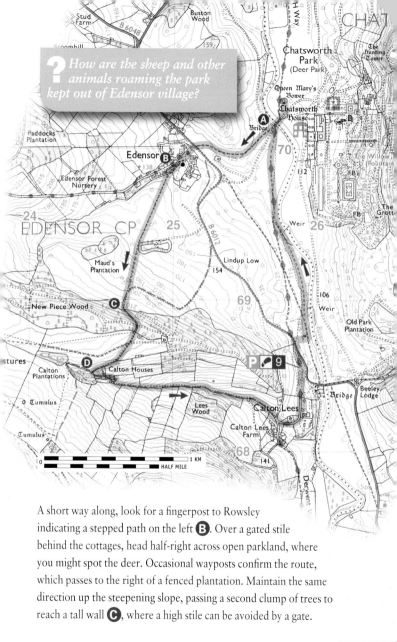

How are the sheep and other animals roaming the park kept out of Edensor village?

A short way along, look for a fingerpost to Rowsley indicating a stepped path on the left **B**. Over a gated stile behind the cottages, head half-right across open parkland, where you might spot the deer. Occasional wayposts confirm the route, which passes to the right of a fenced plantation. Maintain the same direction up the steepening slope, passing a second clump of trees to reach a tall wall **C**, where a high stile can be avoided by a gate.

*The front view of Chatsworth House*

A broad track rises through the wood, turning at the crest to emerge from the trees and reveal a fine view across the Calton Valley. Follow the ongoing path downfield, ignoring a crossing grass track. Approaching a wall at the bottom, follow it right, shortly coming to a gate **D**.

A descending bridleway winds past the cottages of Calton Houses to continue along the base of the valley. Carry on for ½ mile (800m), eventually reaching a junction at Calton Lees Farm. Walk ahead, now on a lane, which soon winds past a garden centre back to the car park. ■

# Monk's Dale and the Limestone Way

- Limestone plateau
- old railway
- National Nature Reserve
- resurgent river

*Monk's Dale is one of several important nature reserves within the National Park, noted for its ancient woodland and hillside meadows. The walk begins from a former railway station, taking an old track between the patchwork of upland fields to the head of the valley. The way back meanders by an intermittent stream and is particularly enjoyable during the spring.*

*walk 10*

Knot Low from Monksdale Farm

# walk 10

**START** Miller's Dale

**DISTANCE** 4¼ miles (6.8km)

**TIME** 2 hours

**PARKING** Miller's Dale station car park (Pay and Display)

**ROUTE FEATURES** Field tracks and rugged woodland paths; moderate ascent; rocky paths may be slippery when wet

**GPS WAYPOINTS**
- SK 138 732
- Ⓐ SK 142 733
- Ⓑ SK 144 734
- Ⓒ SK 136 752
- Ⓓ SK 136 740

**PUBLIC TRANSPORT** Bus service to Miller's Dale

**REFRESHMENTS** Café by car park and pub in Miller's Dale

**PUBLIC TOILETS** At start

**ORDNANCE SURVEY MAPS** Explorer OL24 (The Peak District – White Peak area)

Follow the Monsal Trail left from the old station platforms at Miller's Dale, which crosses the River Wye on one of two parallel bridges to continue along the valley. After ¼ mile (400m) look for a path, marked by a signpost, dropping off the embankment to a footbridge across the river Ⓐ.

Miller's Dale station lay on the Midland Railway line between Buxton and Matlock. Its construction in the middle of the 19th century enabled a vast market for the area's limestone and several huge quarries and lime kilns sprang up along the valley. The line eventually closed in 1968 but was reopened in 1981 as the **Monsal Trail**, a recreational route for walkers and cyclists.

Walk out to a lane and follow it left, passing an information board beside the remains of Miller's Dale meal mill and its 14-foot waterwheel. Reaching the B6049 go right, crossing to then bear left up a steep, narrow lane. A short distance along, double back left up a sharply climbing track, which is marked as the Limestone Way Ⓑ. One of the long-distance paths through the area, it runs between Matlock and Castleton.

The increasing height opens a fine view across the foot of Monk's Dale to the station and the flat-topped summit of Knot Low, while over

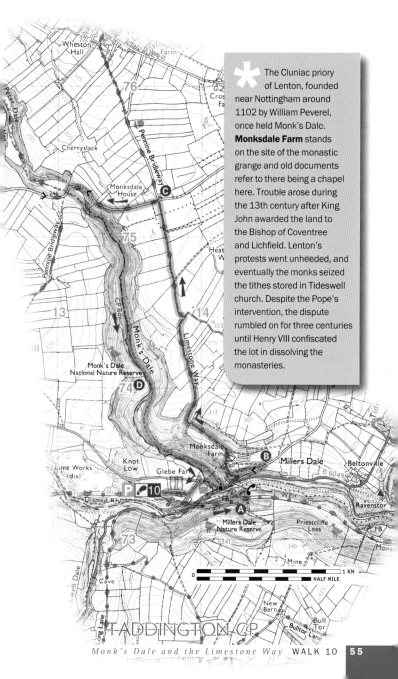

The Cluniac priory of Lenton, founded near Nottingham around 1102 by William Peverel, once held Monk's Dalc. **Monksdale Farm** stands on the site of the monastic grange and old documents refer to there being a chapel here. Trouble arose during the 13th century after King John awarded the land to the Bishop of Coventree and Lichfield. Lenton's protests went unheeded, and eventually the monks seized the tithes stored in Tideswell church. Despite the Pope's intervention, the dispute rumbled on for three centuries until Henry VIII confiscated the lot in dissolving the monasteries.

to the left are the gaunt cliffs of one of the old quarries.

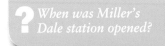

**?** *When was Miller's Dale station opened?*

Beyond a gate, walk through the yard of Monksdale Farm. Leave on the left and resume the climb along a walled track. This soon swings right above a side valley and continues across the undulating upland plateau. Reaching a junction, keep left, the green lane soon beginning a gradual descent between geometric small fields.

Meeting a lane opposite Monksdale House Farm **C**, go left into the valley. Leave at the bottom of the dip through a stile on the left. Head across pasture into the narrow confines of Monk's Dale, a rocky path winding on through the trees. Here in its upper reaches, the stream usually runs below ground and the steep slopes of the valley shelter a dense ash wood. In spring, the dank, mossy understorey is full of wild flowers, which appear before the leaf canopy blocks out the sun's light. Lower down, the stream emanates from the rock and the path eventually breaks from the trees **D**.

Monk's Dale

*A drystone wall on the Limestone Way near Monksdale House*

Continue across the steep slope of a scrub meadow, the climb rewarded with a view along the dale. Later delving back into wood, the way drops to a bridge. On the far bank, take the rocky path rising through the scrub. At the top of the slope carry on beside a wall behind Glebe Farm to a kissing-gate, from which an enclosed path leads to a lane. The car park lies just a short distance down the hill.

# Langsett Reservoir

■ Heather moors     ■ reservoir shorepath
■ ruined farm       ■ far-reaching views

*From a restored 15th-century barn, the walk begins through woodland plantations above the Langsett Reservoir. After crossing the Little Don River, it climbs onto Hingcliff Common. Winding past an abandoned farmstead, the route returns beside more forest to cross the dam back to the start.*

**walk 11**

The ruins of North America Farm

# walk 11

| | |
|---|---|
| **START** | Langsett Barn |
| **DISTANCE** | 3¾ miles (6km) |
| **TIME** | 2 hours |
| **PARKING** | Langsett Barn |

**ROUTE FEATURES** Good
wood and moorland
paths with short stretch
along quiet lane; steady
climb onto Hingcliff
Common

**GPS WAYPOINTS**

- ✎ SE 210 004
- Ⓐ SE 197 005
- Ⓑ SK 202 997
- Ⓒ SK 213 995
- Ⓓ SE 216 000

**PUBLIC TRANSPORT** Bus
service to Langsett

**REFRESHMENTS** Café, pub
and picnic area near
Langsett Barn

**PUBLIC TOILETS** At start

**ORDNANCE SURVEY MAPS**
Explorer OL1 (The Peak
District – Dark Peak
area)

✎ Leave the south-western corner of the
car park, choosing the narrower footpath
rather than the bridleway. Keep left where it
splits, descending through trees towards the
lake. Reaching a lower path, follow it right
below Langsett Bank.

Approaching the head of the reservoir, the
path angles uphill, exchanging the mature
forest for a more recent planting of deciduous
wood. At a fork, branch left joining a broader
track that drops to Brookhouse Bridge. It
spans The Porter, which is also known as the
Little Don River.

On the far bank Ⓐ, swing left through a
gate, the path winding steeply uphill beside
more forest. Leaving the trees behind, the
gradient eases and the way continues across
the open heather and bilberry moor flanking
Hingcliff Hill. A ¼ mile (400m) walk leads to
a prominent fork, which stands at the highest
point of the circuit, some 1,100 feet (335m)
above sea level.

> ❓ Using GPS or map and
> romer, determine the grid
> reference of the walk's high
> point on Hingcliff Common.

Take the left branch, which soon begins a
gentle descent, eventually reaching the fallen

stones of a ruined steading, North America Farm. Carry on through a gate **B**, the path dropping more steeply beside Mauk Royd plantation. Cross the foot of Thickwoods Brook, staying with the main track as it swings left beside the water and then right, rising to a metal gate.

> The distinctive call of the **red grouse** is likely to be heard before the birds are seen, though their low curving flight is one of the most evocative sights of the moors. The patchwork of heather seen on this walk demonstrates how moorland management works. The long patches provide cover for nesting and shelter, while the newly burned areas give the grouse their favourite food – young heather shoots.

The way continues as Thickwoods Lane, a rough trail through the trees. Passing through another gate, keep going on a concrete track to meet the corner of a lane **C**.

However, ignore the tarmac and instead take the rising track off to the left, which leads to the handful of stone cottages at Upper Midhope. Go

> When dams were built in the 19th century, the land in the direct catchment was cleared to help ensure water purity. **North America Farm** was one such casualty, with the buildings abandoned and the livestock moved to avoid the danger of pollution. Aforestation of the banks was undertaken for the same purpose and had the added benefit of producing a cash crop of timber. Today, there are water purification plants so the surrounding moors can be opened to the public.

left and follow the track to a farm gate, there turning right before it on a footpath beside a wall. It falls easily to meet a lane at the bottom **D**. Turn left, continuing across the Langsett Dam.

At the far side, you can remain with the lane, climbing past the grand-looking valve house to the main road. There go left to the Wagon and Horses and turn in beside it. At the top of the yard, wander between stone cottages to find a path back past

Langsett Barn to the car park. *Alternatively, if you are not looking for refreshment, take the path left below the valve house. Beyond a gate climb back up to the car park.* ■

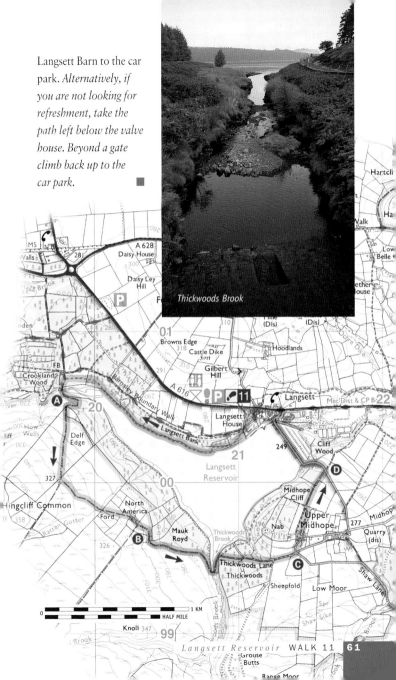

*Thickwoods Brook*

# Youlgrave and the River Lathkill

■ Trout streams
■ limestone crags
■ riverside paths
■ high plateau meadows

*walk 12*

This enjoyable walk, centred on the pretty White Peak village of Youlgrave, takes in two of the area's best known trout streams and contrasts the lower lush meadows with the craggy walls enclosing their higher reaches. The path linking the two valleys crosses the high plateau meadows, opening a wide panorama across the landscape.

Lathkill Dale below Over Haddon

# walk 12

From the Bull's Head in the centre of Youlgrave, walk down the main street past 19th-century Fountain, a water tank that furnished the village water supply. Turn left into Holywell Lane, descending to the River Bradford and follow the riverbank downstream, watching for trout in the clear water.

*Both the River Bradford, which is barely 2 miles (3.2km) long, and the River Lathkill into which it flows, are renowned **trout streams**. Way back in the 17th century, Charles Cotton, who contributed to Izaak Walton's famous work, *The Compleat Angler,* said the Lathkill was 'by many degrees, the purest and most transparent stream that I ever yet saw, either at home or abroad.'

At the end, walk out to a lane Ⓐ and cross to a gate opposite. The ongoing path curves left then switches onto the south bank. Ignore a small, arched bridge and remain with the track below the vertical crag of Rhienstor. Where it subsequently turns away, keep ahead through a gate to carry on along the valley, where drifts of meadowsweet, cranesbill and scabious speckle summer meadows. The path later leads out to a lane at Alport Ⓑ.

Cross by a telephone box and take the footpath opposite signed to Conksbury. The way continues beside successive meadows, the

River Lathkill lying to the right but not always visible. You will eventually arrive at a crossing track near Raper Lodge **C**.

Here, you can make a brief diversion along the track to a bridge across the river, above which, a curving weir holds back a deep trout pool. The fish are huge but you are asked not to feed them as it impairs breeding.

Return to carry on along the footpath, shortly meeting a lane at Conksbury. Watching for oncoming traffic, follow it down to Conksbury Bridge. Cross the river to find a footpath off left on the far bank **D**.

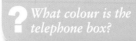

**? What colour is the telephone box?**

The rock beneath your feet is **Carboniferous limestone**, which is soluble in the slight acidity of rainwater. Over time, seeping water widens minute cracks until, eventually, it creates underwater channels sufficiently large to swallow the river. The water continues underground until it meets an impervious layer of rock, when it is forced back to the surface in a resurgence. Vanishing and re-appearing rivers are one of the most fascinating features of limestone country.

*River Lathkill near Conksbury Bridge*

The path heads upstream beside woodland and a narrow strip of waterside meadow, while the river itself is stepped in a series of weirs that create pools for the trout. Approaching Lathkill Lodge the valley narrows and, after a spell of little rain, it can be a surprise to find the riverbed dry.

Reaching a bridge **E** cross to the southern bank and climb away left on a steadily rising track that twists back to a gate at the top. To the left a path

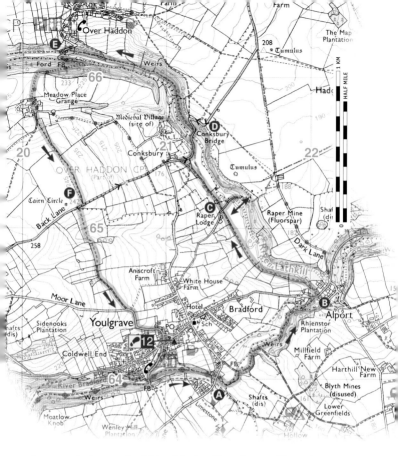

is waymarked across the field to Meadow Place Grange. Through gates, pass between barns into an extensive yard. Walk straight across, leaving the courtyard beside the end building to the field behind. Climb away, closing with a wall on the left. Remain with it at the edge of a second field to meet Back Lane **F**.

Turn right, but then almost immediately abandon it for a path signed off left. Pass through a couple of squeeze-stiles and cross the head of a shallow valley. Meeting the end of a rough track, follow it out to Moor Lane. It is then just a short walk down the hill back to Youlgrave. ∎

# Thor's Cave and Beeston Tor

- ▇ Impressive cave
- ▇ limestone scenery
- ▇ Manifold Way
- ▇ towering crags

*walk 13*

*Thor's Cave is one of the dramatic features of the White Peak and is visited on this scenic walk from the village of Wetton. The middle section follows the line of the old Manifold railway through a lovely gorge before climbing back across fields to the village.*

*Beeston Tor*

# walk 13

**START** Wetton

**DISTANCE** 3¾ miles (6km)

**TIME** 2 hours

**PARKING** Wetton car park

**ROUTE FEATURES**
Farmland and riverside
paths and tracks; some
steep, stepped ascents

**GPS WAYPOINTS**
SK 109 551
Ⓐ SK 106 552
Ⓑ SK 098 551
Ⓒ SK 100 541
Ⓓ SK 105 540
Ⓔ SK 104 543

**PUBLIC TRANSPORT**
Infrequent bus service to
Wetton

**REFRESHMENTS** Pub in
Wetton

**PUBLIC TOILETS** At start

**ORDNANCE SURVEY MAPS**
Explorer OL24 (The Peak
District – White Peak
area))

Over a stile at the village end of the car park, follow a gently rising track to a farm. Walk out through the yard to a lane and go left to a road junction Ⓐ.

Bear right but after 30 yards, fork off left along a walled track, marked as a concessionary footpath to Thor's Cave. Prominent ahead beyond the wooded cleft of the Manifold Valley is the tall spire of Grindon church.

Pass through a gate, but after 50 yards, look for a fingerpost marking a stile on the right. Cross and go left by the wall, passing through another gate, beyond which the path becomes clearer and soon leads to Thor's Cave.

Thor was the **Norse god of thunder** and it is possible that this imposing gash was named after him, although more likely it derives from the word 'tor', meaning a rocky outcrop. Excavations suggest Thor's Cave was intermittently occupied from some 10,000 years ago to the time of the Romans, making it one of the earliest known human sites in the Peak. Several prehistoric burials have been discovered as well as artefacts and animal bones.

Take the stepped path from the mouth of the cave, which descends across the wooded hillside to a junction. Go left and continue down to a footbridge across the river Ⓑ.

Follow the Manifold Way to the left, eventually emerging through a small car park onto a lane beside Weag's Bridge **C**.

**?** *What prehistoric animal bones have been found in Thor's Cave?*

*You can shorten the walk and avoid the stepping stones farther downstream, although the river is usually dry at that point, by following the lane over the bridge and up the hill to a cattle-grid near* **E** *.*

The main route, however, continues down the valley along the right-hand one of the two lanes opposite. The towering crag of Beeston Tor soon comes into view ahead. After some 500 yards cross a stile on the left onto the adjacent farm access road and follow it over a bridge crossing the mouth of the River Hamps.

After 50 yards, watch for a fingerpost pointing through a wooden gate on the left **D** to stepping stones beneath the rocky outcrop of Beeston Tor. *Although the river has normally disappeared underground by this point, heavy rain can occasionally submerge the stepping stones. In which case you should retreat to Weag's Bridge and follow the alternative route.*

On the far bank, go left for 20 yards to a stile. Walk forward to a fingerpost, which indicates a well-graded path rising along a grassy shelf to a gate and squeeze-stile. Bear right and follow a wall out to a lane, there joining the alternative route by a cattle-grid.

A few yards beyond the cattle-grid, between two gateways on the left is a

**\*** Created in 1937 by Staffordshire County Council, the **Manifold Way** follows the disused Leek and Manifold Light Railway. The single-track line carried farm produce and tourists, but had only a brief existence between 1904 and 1934. It is now enjoyed by cyclists and walkers following the winding river.

waymarked stile **E**. Head steeply upfield to a meet a second lane and carry on along it up the hill. After 200 yards, leave over a stile on the left and strike out half-right towards the buildings of Wetton, coming into view ahead.

Carry on across successive fields, aiming just left of the tower of Wetton's church. Approaching a farm, pass left of the buildings

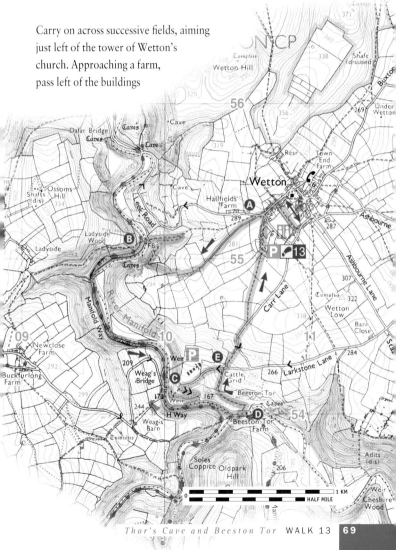

and look for a stile in the corner by the farmhouse. Walk along the edge of its garden to emerge at a road junction. Retrace your outward route back to the car park. ■

Thor's Cave

# Torside Reservoir

- Pennine Way
- Longdendale Trail
- gritstone scenery
- high dams

*This walk, which circles the Torside Reservoir, begins and ends along the Longdendale Trail, a former railway. There is a succession of inspiring views from both sides of the valley and an enjoyable saunter for the final leg.*

*walk 14*

*The Torside Reservoir overspill*

# walk 14

**START** Torside Visitor
Centre, beside B6105;
*alternative start at
Crowden*

**DISTANCE** 4¼ miles (6.8km)

**TIME** 2 hours

**PARKING** Car parks at
Torside and Crowden

**ROUTE FEATURES** Paths
and tracks; a couple
of steep flights of
descending steps

**GPS WAYPOINTS**
🔲 SK 068 983
Ⓐ SK 080 992
🔲 SK 072 992 (Alt start)
Ⓑ SK 071 994
Ⓒ SK 060 986
Ⓓ SK 057 980

**PUBLIC TRANSPORT**
Seasonal bus service to
Torside

**REFRESHMENTS** Seasonal
café at visitor centre

**PUBLIC TOILETS** Torside
and Crowden car parks

**ORDNANCE SURVEY MAPS**
Explorer OL1 (The Peak
District – Dark Peak
area)

🥾 A clear path from the rear of the car
park climbs past a memorial woodland to the
Longdendale Trail. To the left, it runs easily
for almost ½ mile (800m) before drawing
close to the road. Watch for a path signed
to Crowden falling back to the left Ⓐ. At
the bottom, cross the road to a gate opposite
and continue down a broad track to meet an
outflow channel below the Woodhead Dam.

Bear left across a footbridge then descend a
steep flight of steps to a lower path, which
leads away beside a concrete water
channel. Ignore a low bridge and carry
on to a kissing-gate at the end of the
path, there turning right to the
A628 trans-Pennine road.

Follow the footway
right for some 50
yards before
carefully
crossing
to a

side road. Walk up past the entrance of the Crowden car park *(the alternative start)* to a junction at the top. Turn left to reach a second junction **B**, where, if you go left past

How long did it take to construct the Woodhead Railway?

Hey Edge

the Camping and Caravanning Club site, you will find toilets.

The onward route, however, lies ahead past a large barn and farm. After crossing Crowden Brook the track makes for higher ground, opening views to the dark hills. The steep slopes culminate in a long line of rugged edges, behind which, desolate moors roll back to Bleaklow Hill, the second highest top of the Peakland hills.

A gentle descent brings you back to the main road **C**. Be vigilant crossing to a gate

**The Trans-Pennine Trail** runs for 215 miles (346km) coast to coast between Southport and Hornsea, and here follows the former Woodhead Railway. The line opened in 1845 and was the first to be pushed across the Pennine wilderness, providing a link between the manufacturing cities of Manchester and Sheffield. The summit section passed through a 3-mile (4.8-km), single track tunnel, which, when built, was one of the longest in the world. A second tunnel was soon added to accommodate increasing traffic. A third, two-way tunnel opened in 1953 when the line was electrified. Despite the investment, the line closed in 1981 and one of the Victorian tunnels now carries the power cables that snake up the valley, protecting them from the fierce winter storms that batter the watershed.

opposite. A path falls past Tinsel School Wood and wanders right through a pleasant strip of pinewood above the Torside Reservoir.

Finally emerging from the trees, drop to a track. Cross that and a parallel concrete water channel to continue down steps to the main service road. Follow it over the dam, climbing left on the other side.

Approaching the top of the track, double back right to the B6105 **D**. Cross and go left along the Trans-Pennine Trail. Where it shortly forks, take the left branch, which is marked for pedestrians and cyclists. The course of a former railway, the track meanders pleasantly up the valley, taking you across the foot of Torside Clough. This dark rift bites deep into the moors, conveniently ushering the Pennine Way off the bare wastes of Bleaklow Head. Another ½ mile (800m) of walking brings you to a junction, where the path left returns you to the car park. ■

*The Trans-Pennine Trail*

# Monuments on the Eastern Moors

- Gritstone edges
- great views
- monuments
- rock outcrops

walk 15

*Birchen Edge overlooks the valley of Bar Brook above Baslow. On top there are striking monuments to England's greatest historical naval commander, Nelson, while across on the tip of Baslow Edge, Wellington is similarly commemorated. The walk also touches on history of a different sort, following stretches of packhorse route, the motorways of a long-gone age.*

The Three Ships

**START** Birchen Edge car park

**DISTANCE** 4½ miles (7.2km)

**TIME** 2 hours

**PARKING** Birchen Edge car park, off A619 near the Robin Hood Inn; do not use pub car park

**ROUTE FEATURES** Moorland paths with some moderate ascents; dogs must be kept on a lead

**GPS WAYPOINTS**
- 🗺 SK 280 720
- Ⓐ SK 281 722
- Ⓑ SK 278 731
- Ⓒ SK 276 740
- Ⓓ SK 262 736
- Ⓔ SK 260 734
- Ⓕ SK 268 733
- Ⓖ SK 277 721

**PUBLIC TRANSPORT** Bus service to Robin Hood

**REFRESHMENTS** Robin Hood Inn at start, pubs and tearooms at nearby Baslow

**PUBLIC TOILETS** In Baslow

**ORDNANCE SURVEY MAPS** Explorer OL24 (The Peak District – White Peak area)

👢 From the car park, walk away from the Robin Hood Inn along the B6050. After 50 yards turn left through a gate onto the Access Land of the Eastern Moors Estate, from which a sandy path leads through bracken and birch.

The main path simply runs ahead below the crags, missing the best of the views. However, 200 yards along, look for a rocky path leaving on the right near a large boulder Ⓐ. After a steep, but short pull, it swings north to rise more easily along the edge, weaving between the heather and gritstone boulders. The views across the valley during the next ½ mile (800m) are superb, but the eye is inevitably drawn towards a slender column topped by a ball, perched on the cliff edge ahead.

✳ A local businessman erected the pillar in 1810, just five years after Nelson's death from a sniper's bullet at the Battle of Trafalgar. The **three massive boulders** nearby, named for his ships, honour the successes of Nelson at the battles of the Nile in 1798 and Trafalgar in 1805.

Continue past the monument to the concrete triangulation pillar, which marks the high point of the edge at 1,017 feet (310m) Ⓑ.

Having savoured the view and spotted your next objective across the valley, look for a

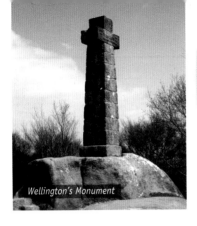
Wellington's Monument

**?** *What are the Three Ships called?*

path dropping left from the trig column through a heathery gully. Meeting a broader path, follow it right in gentle descent across the moor, where occasional sections of flagstones alleviate the wettest stretches. It ends at a gate near a crossroads. Go left, carefully crossing the main A621 to the lane opposite. Leave after 150 yards through a gate on the left **C**.

A firm and level track carries the onward route to the edge of more moorland above a birch wood that falls into the deepening valley below. It is in fact an old road, evidenced by an ancient guidepost marked 'Chesterfeild Roade'. An easy ¾ mile (1.2km) leads to the Wellington monument, a sturdy cross perched on a sprawling boulder.

Carry on to a prominent junction a little farther on **D**, divert right to visit the Eagle Stone.

Return to the junction **D** and keep ahead with the main path, passing below disused quarries before winding down to a gate **E**. Do not go through but instead turn sharp left beside the wall along a waymarked path at the foot of a bracken-covered slope. Entering oak wood, the path continues between moss-covered

**\*** Following the great victory at the Battle of Waterloo in 1815, a local doctor by the name of Wrench felt that his hero was as equally worthy of recognition as Nelson and caused this monument to be erected to the first **Duke of Wellington**. It too occupies a superb viewpoint overlooking Baslow, while to the south is the parkland of the Chatsworth estate.

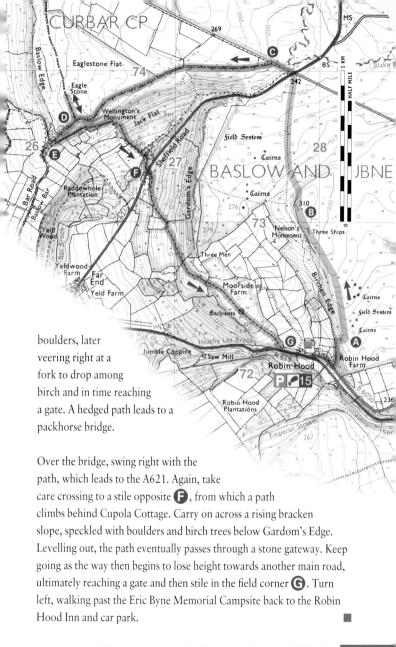

boulders, later
veering right at a
fork to drop among
birch and in time reaching
a gate. A hedged path leads to
a packhorse bridge.

Over the bridge, swing right with the
path, which leads to the A621. Again, take
care crossing to a stile opposite **F**, from which a path
climbs behind Cupola Cottage. Carry on across a rising bracken
slope, speckled with boulders and birch trees below Gardom's Edge.
Levelling out, the path eventually passes through a stone gateway. Keep
going as the way then begins to lose height towards another main road,
ultimately reaching a gate and then stile in the field corner **G**. Turn
left, walking past the Eric Byne Memorial Campsite back to the Robin
Hood Inn and car park.

# Ladybower Reservoir and Cutthroat Bridge

- ■ Heather moorland
- ■ reservoir setting
- ■ lovely views
- ■ lost village

*walk 16*

*Beginning at the Ashopton Viaduct this walk ascends the wooded slopes flanking Lead Hill to a magnificent viewpoint. After an enjoyable ramble across heather moorland to Cutthroat Bridge, the final leg follows an old packhorse trail, passing above the Ladybower Inn and opening final views to Bamford Edge and Win Hill.*

*Ladybower Reservoir from Whinstone Lee Fields*

# walk 16

**START** A57, east of Ashopton Viaduct

**DISTANCE** 3¾ miles (6km)

**TIME** 2 hours

**PARKING** Parking beside A57 just east of Ashopton Viaduct

**ROUTE FEATURES** Clear moorland paths and tracks; strenuous ascent

**GPS WAYPOINTS**

🔲 SK 196 864
🅐 SK 198 865
🅑 SK 197 873
🅒 SK 213 875
🅓 SK 205 865

**PUBLIC TRANSPORT** Bus service to Ashopton

**REFRESHMENTS** Ladybower Inn, picnic tables at Heatherdene

**PUBLIC TOILETS** At nearby Heatherdene

**ORDNANCE SURVEY MAPS** Explorer OL1 (The Peak District – Dark Peak area)

🔲 Follow the main road towards the Ashopton Viaduct, carefully crossing just before it to turn off onto a rising tarmac track. Keep right around a sharp bend, climbing above a house and past a forest maintenance yard. Higher up the track degrades to gravel, eventually ending through a gate in a small enclosure beside a small, covered reservoir 🅐.

Through a small gate on the left follow a clear path signed to Whinstone Lee Tor that cuts back uphill among larches. Reaching a fork, keep left by the wall. The gradient soon eases and shortly the trees give way to an expansive view along the Upper Derwent Valley. Just across the water are the distinctive twin tops of Crook Hill.

Before long, the climb resumes, at first beside the wall and then breaking away to rise more strenuously. Higher up swing right again, the path making a determined final assault up a hollow way that soon broaches the ridge near a silver National Trust sign.

**?** *What name is on the National Trust sign?*

At the junction there 🅑, walk a short distance to the right to reach a superb vantage

---

above the valley. Win Hill rises above the opposite shore of Ladybower Reservoir, while Lose Hill and the distant mass of Kinder Scout can be seen farther west. Behind you, the lonely moors fall gradually towards Sheffield,

surprisingly only some 7 miles (11km) away.

Return to the crossing **B** and now bear right on a clear path. It is the path that lies almost opposite the one up which you climbed and descends gently due east across the open moor.

*Looking north from Ashopton Woods, Upper Derwent*

After ¾ mile (1.2km), the trail curves left, then drops more steeply through a sharp right-hand bend into Highshaw Clough. Just before you pass under electricity cables, bear off right onto a narrower path **C**. It veers right above Cutthroat Bridge, joining a second path to continue high above the road at the edge of the moor.

Fording a stream, the track passes through a gate into the Ladybower Wood Nature

Reserve. This natural sessile oak wood is one of the few remaining such areas in the Peak District, a remnant of habitat that once spread over much of the uplands.

Eventually leaving the reserve, carry on to a fork **D**. Just ahead lies the Ladybower Inn, but the way back is to the right, signed to Ashopton. Pass

The Ladybower is the largest of the three reservoirs cradled in the **Upper Derwent Valley** and, opened by King George VI in 1945, was the last to be constructed. However, it was a sad day for those whose homes had been in the tiny villages of Derwent and Ashopton, which were swallowed up beneath the rising waters. A new estate to re-house the evacuees was built at Yorkshire Bridge, in the valley just below the massive dam.

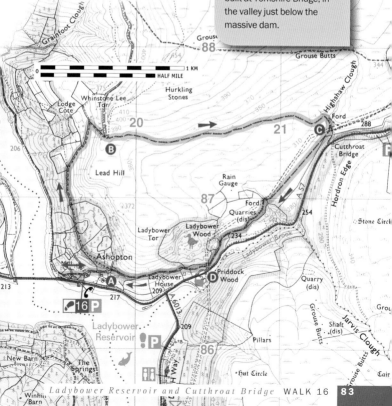

behind the pub and, emerging from oak wood, climb beside a drystone wall. Remain with the wall to crest the rise, where the view opens once more to reveal the prominent profile of Bamford Edge running away to the south. Returning to the grassy enclosure **A**, keep ahead to retrace your outward route to the main road. ■

Below Whinstone Lee Tor

# Hayfield and Lantern Pike

- Rolling moorland
- attractive village
- summit viewfinder
- old mill

*Sheltered within the folds of the western Peak, Hayfield is an attractive start point for this exhilarating walk onto the surrounding moors. It takes in the historic Snake Path, a converted textile mill and a grand viewpoint, finishing with an easy stroll along the course of an old railway.*

*walk* **17**

Hayfield from Lantern Pike

**START** Hayfield

**DISTANCE** 5 miles (8km)

**TIME** 2½ hours

**PARKING** Car park at former Hayfield station (Pay and Display)

**ROUTE FEATURES** Moorland paths and tracks; several steep ascents

**GPS WAYPOINTS**
- 🥾 SK 036 869
- Ⓐ SK 045 880
- Ⓑ SK 034 881
- Ⓒ SK 026 885
- Ⓓ SK 024 874
- Ⓔ SK 021 868

**PUBLIC TRANSPORT** Bus services to Hayfield

**REFRESHMENTS** Kiosk and picnic tables at start; café at Birch Vale; pubs and cafés in Hayfield

**PUBLIC TOILETS** At start

**ORDNANCE SURVEY MAPS** Explorer OL1 (The Peak District – Dark Peak area)

🥾 Cross the main road at the pedestrian traffic lights opposite the car park entrance. Walk beside the Conservative Club and St Matthew's Church to the town's main street next to the Bull's Head.

Go left across the River Sett, turning right on the bend just beyond the bridge into Bank Street. Bear right as it then merges with Kinder Road, climbing past rows of characterful stone cottages that are typical of this former textile village. After some 300 yards, watch for the Snake Path leaving between houses on the left. A famous right of way dedicated in 1897, it rises steeply as a track, swinging right to pass through a couple of restored metal kissing-gates and later passing above a prominent clump of trees standing in isolation upon the hillside grazing.

Degrading to a path, the way remains clear as the gradient eases, eventually passing through a couple of gates onto the open moor of the National Trust's High Peak estate. Ahead, the massive plateau of Kinder Scout fills the skyline, culminating in Kinder Low to the right. The high point of the great hill, however, lies hidden a further ½ mile (800m) to the north-west, although it is barely 19 feet (5.8m) higher.

Carry on beside a wall for 75 yards to find, just before its end, a narrow path turning off

*On top of Lantern Pike*

sharp left **A**. It weaves through heather on the fringe of Middle Moor, then angles downhill through bracken and rhododendrons to a wall surrounding the grounds of Park Hall. Pass through a gate into Park Hall Woods and swing left onto a wide track among mature trees. The way gently descends to meet the main road at Little Hayfield **B**.

Carefully cross the busy A624 and continue down Slack Lane opposite to an old mill that has been converted into apartments. Immediately beyond the mill, turn right across two bridges, briefly following the stream to a stile. A stone causey tackles a grassy slope before the path turns by an old hawthorn hedge to rise towards an ivy-covered house. Over stiles, cross its drive and continue up a sunken track.

There are fine views back across the valley as the path gains height to a stile by the top corner of a wood. Mounting that, bear left on a clear path rising over a grassy shoulder, which is pocked with old coal workings, before curving left down to a gate **C**.

Climb the rough track to a second gate, passing through onto the National Trust's landholding. Just beyond, branch off onto a path, which progresses steeply through the heather to the top of Lantern Pike.

From the summit, continue along the ridge to a meet a drystone wall and swing left beside it, tilting in sharp descent to rejoin the main track. Turn right through a gate and walk down to reach a minor road **D**.

Go right, but immediately bear off left on a downhill track signed to Hegginbottom Farm. Reaching a hairpin bend, keep ahead through a small gate onto a pleasant old path, which drops through the trees to end by old stone weavers' cottages at Birch Vale above the River Sett.

Turn left across the river, passing the Special Touch Café to find a gate on the left **E**, through which the Pennine Bridleway is signed to Hayfield. The track briefly parallels the lane before twisting

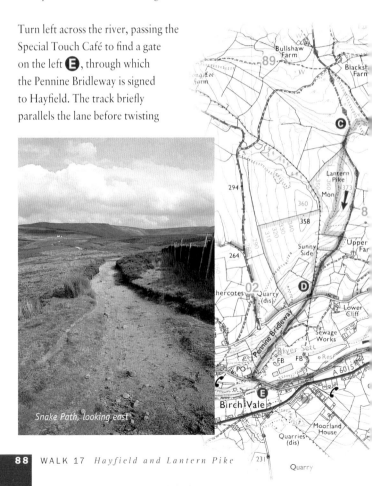

Snake Path, looking east

to settle along the course of the former railway. A mile (1.6km) of easy and pleasant walking along the valley takes you back to the car park. ∎

Lantern Pike reputedly gets its name from the fact that there was once a warning beacon on the top. The hill was purchased and donated to the National Trust in 1950 in memory of one of the early footpath activists, **Edwin Royce**, and commemorates his 'labour in the cause of securing the freedom of the hills'. There is a superb view, particularly to the south-east over Hayfield and the peat-covered plateau of Kinder Scout beyond. A topograph helps identify the various hills to be seen around the skyline.

**?** *In which direction does Kinder Scout lie from the summit of Lantern Pike?*

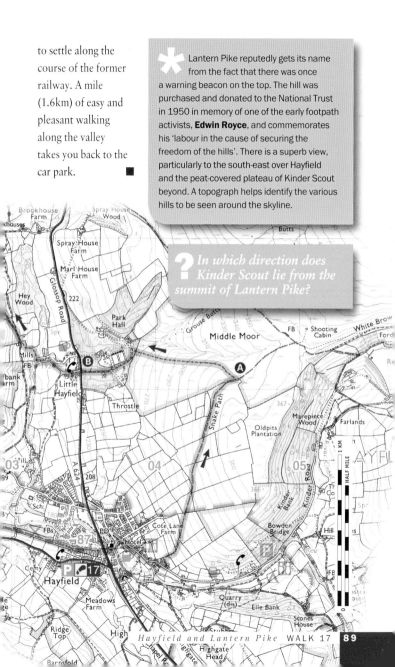

# The Goyt Valley and Windgather Rocks

- Reservoirs
- heather moorland
- craggy outcrops
- waterside woodland

*walk 18*

*The Goyt Valley is one of the most popular areas in the Peak District, but this walk explores one of its less frequented corners above the Fernilee Reservoir before climbing back past the striking gritstone outcrop of Windgather Rocks, a favourite spot for rock climbers.*

*Across the Goyt Valley*

# walk 18

**START** Errwood Reservoir; *alternative start Pym Chair*

**DISTANCE** 5½ miles (8.9km)

**TIME** 3 hours

**PARKING** Car parks at The Street (by Errwood Reservoir) or Pym Chair

**FEATURES** Clear tracks and moorland paths; strenuous ascent

**GPS WAYPOINTS**
* SK 013 756
Ⓐ SK 012 776
Ⓑ SK 007 783
Ⓒ SK 003 786
Ⓓ SJ 999 786
Ⓔ SJ 994 783
Ⓕ SJ 995 771
* SJ 994 767 (Alt start)

**PUBLIC TRANSPORT** None

**REFRESHMENTS** Picnic tables at The Street

**PUBLIC TOILETS** At Bunsal Cob, ½ mile (800m) east of The Street

**ORDNANCE SURVEY MAPS** Explorer OL24 (The Peak District – White Peak area)

👣 From the junction by the car park, take the lane signed over the Errwood Dam to Buxton. However, leave after only a few yards along a path indicated off left towards a gate. Bear half-right, dropping past a waypost and through a second gate into woodland overlooking the head of the Fernilee Reservoir. A narrow path tilts down to meet a broader track, which then runs on above the shore.

> ✳ The **Fernilee Reservoir** is one of two nestling in the main fold of the Goyt Valley. It was built by Stockport Water Corporation to supply drinking water to the town and was completed in 1938. Immediately above is the somewhat smaller Errwood Reservoir, a relative newcomer as it was only completed in 1967.

After ½ mile (800m), at a red marker, the path leaves the waterside and climbs a flight of steps. Reaching a track beside a wall, follow it right, still in the forest, towards Fernilee. Eventually emerging from the trees through a gate, head along a metalled track down to the Fernilee Dam Ⓐ, from which point there is an impressive view back along the reservoir.

> ❓ *What are the places named on the cast-iron footpath sign?*

However, do not cross the dam, instead bear left and continue along the side of the valley, later reaching Knipe Farm.

There, the track swings left into Mill Clough to meet the stream tumbling at its base. After crossing the flow on a hairpin bend **B**, carry on up towards Madscar Farm. Bear left past the entrance with the main track, here marked as the Midshires Way. It then shortly twists through another hairpin up to Overton Hall Farm. Keep ahead past the farm, climbing to Taxal Moor Road at the top **C**.

A fingerpost indicates a path directly opposite, which continues the ascent straight up the hill onto the moor beside the boundary of a forest plantation. At the crest, pause to enjoy the view back to Ladder Hill and Eccles Pike. Reaching a Peak and Northern Footpaths Society cast-iron sign **D**, head half-left down to a ladder-stile.

Briefly follow the edge of the plantation right, the path then delving into the trees. Drop to a boggy dip crossed by a plank and strategically placed log and climb away to find a stile on the left into the wood. Enclosed beside a wall, the way runs at the edge of the trees before it turns up to a gate. Keep ahead onto the crest of Windgather Rocks **E**, from which there is a superb panorama across the Cheshire Plain.

Head south along the edge, the crags ultimately giving out to bring the path beside the lane. Remain with the path for ½ mile (800m) until you reach a stile on the right **F**. *If you have started from Pym Chair, simply keep with the path beside the lane for another ¼ mile (400m).* Otherwise, head east of south, picking up a line of posts that cut a corner of the moor to meet The Street, just east of the Pym Chair car park.

*If starting from Pym Chair, turn left from the car park and go left again at the road junction, picking up a footpath that runs alongside The Street.*

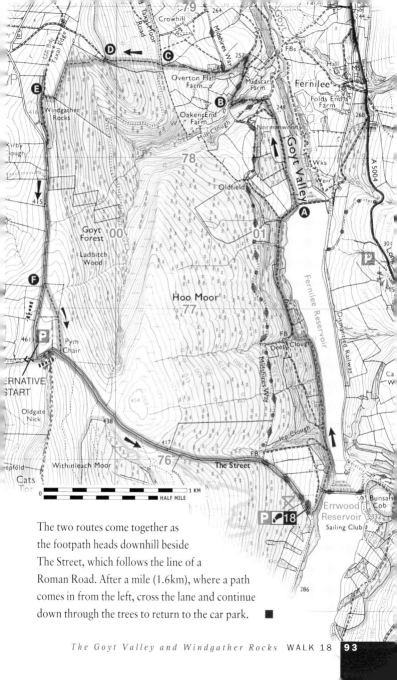

The two routes come together as
the footpath heads downhill beside
The Street, which follows the line of a
Roman Road. After a mile (1.6km), where a path
comes in from the left, cross the lane and continue
down through the trees to return to the car park. ■

# Beresford, Wolfscote and Biggin Dales

- Unspoilt valleys
- trout stream
- limestone upland
- crags and caves

*Beresford and Wolfscote Dales are just two of the White Peak's delightful gorges, but Biggin Dale, although less frequented, has a charm of its own. They are linked here on a walk from Hartington, a market town since 1203 and, until recently, famous for its Dovedale Blue cheese. The Hartington Cheese Shop has been given a new lease of life and continues to sell speciality cheeses.*

Wolfscote Dale

# walk 19

**START** Hartington

**DISTANCE** 5¾ miles (9.3km)

**TIME** 3 hours

**PARKING** Parsons Field car park (Pay and Display)

**ROUTE FEATURES** Field and riverside paths; rocky paths may be slippery when wet

**GPS WAYPOINTS**
- 🖉 SK 127 602
- Ⓐ SK 128 592
- Ⓑ SK 130 584
- Ⓒ SK 142 569
- Ⓓ SK 145 587
- Ⓔ SK 135 595
- Ⓕ SK 131 603

**PUBLIC TRANSPORT** Bus service to Hartington

**REFRESHMENTS** Tearooms and pubs in Hartington

**PUBLIC TOILETS** Alongside Rooke's Pottery near start of walk

**ORDNANCE SURVEY MAPS** Explorer Explorer OL24 (The Peak District – White Peak area)

Walk towards the village from the car park, but almost immediately turn right to a footpath signed between the pottery and public toilets. A clear path leads away at the field edge, eventually meeting a walled track. Over a stile opposite, a trod continues across more pastures, skirting the western flank of a small grassy knoll, Pennilow.

Passing through a gate Ⓐ, the path wanders between trees, shortly joining the banks of the River Dove.

> **?** *According to the plaque, when was this area of woodland planted?*

The path switches onto the western bank, shortly reaching a second footbridge. Cross back and, bearing right, stride out along a meadow. *If the going is wet, head for a stile in the left wall to join a track that runs along the top of the meadow. Go right when you reach a junction to drop back to the river at Frank i' th' Rocks Bridge.*

Ignore the stone bridge at the far end of the meadow Ⓑ and continue along a good path that leads into the confines of Wolfscote Dale. One of the many National Trust holdings in the Peak District, it is impressively overlooked by bare outcrops of stark limestone. Of the two crags to the left, the nearest is Frank's Rock, at the base of which is Frank i' th' Rocks Cave. Excavations there have uncovered the remains of Roman and Anglo-Saxon burials.

Farther on, the valley sides slope back in steep banks of scree, dotted here and there by hardy trees. The river attracts plenty of water birds and heron are a common sight. Eventually, the deep cleft of a small side valley enters the dale on the far side of the river by the prominent buttresses of Drabber Tor, just beyond which are the Peaseland Rocks.

✳ Looking to the right above the river, you might catch a glimpse of **Beresford Tower**, which stands on the site of the now demolished Beresford Hall. It was the home of Charles Cotton, collaborator and friend of Izaak Walton, who penned the famous treatise *The Compleat Angler*. They often fished the river, but the deep pool here, known as Pike Pool is named not for the fish, but the detached pinnacle of limestone, which rises from the water.

Hartington village and pond

Biggin Dale then comes in from the left ⊙. Turn into it, just before a gate, and follow a path along the valley. It has a wilder character than that of Wolfscote Dale and, unless there has been heavy rain, the stream at its base flows below ground. *Nevertheless, the rocky path can be slippery when wet.* Through a gate higher up, pass into the National Nature Reserve, important for the profusion of wild flowers found in its steep, calcareous meadows. Carry on through a second gate, following the line of a wall along the bottom of the fold and later curving around

*Weir, footbridge and meadow, Beresford Dale*

a dew pond to reach a gate **D**.

A signpost points the way along a tributary valley to Hartington. Head up that, but after some 200 yards at another signpost, bear left again for a short energetic pull to a gate. Continue along a walled track, which leads out to a junction of lanes. Take the one ahead, Reynards Lane, leaving after 200 yards over a stile on the right **E**.

Strike half-left, crossing an intervening wall to reach the far corner of a second field. Carry on along a walled green lane, which gently descends past a junction to end opposite Hartington Hall youth hostel **F**. Follow the lane down the hill back into Hartington. ■

The Batemans built **Hartington Hall** in the early Jacobean style in 1611. They came to the area from Norfolk in the previous century. The family remained here until the 1930s after which the house was opened as a youth hostel and it has the distinction of being the first youth hostel in the country to be furnished with electricity and central heating. The hall's other claim to fame is that Bonnie Prince Charlie is reputed to have spent the night here in the Jacobite uprising of 1745 during his foray into England.

# Kinder Scout and Jacob's Ladder

- High peat moorland
- fine views
- dramatic rock outcrops
- ancient routeway

*Although the most 'adventurous' walk in the book, this exploration of Kinder Scout's fringe poses no significant difficulty on a fine day. However, the final ascent of Crowden Clough is steep and somewhat scrambling, but rewarded by magnificent views. Skirting the desolate plateau, boulders sculpted by the elements excite the imagination before returning beside the Rive Noe.*

**walk 20**

Looking east across the Wool Packs, Kinder Scout

**START** Barber Booth

**DISTANCE** 5¾ miles (9.3km)

**TIME** 3 hours

**PARKING** Barber Booth car park

**ROUTE FEATURES**
Rugged moorland paths, strenuous climbs and a steep descent; *unsuitable for inexperienced walkers in poor weather*; dogs must be kept on a lead

**GPS WAYPOINTS**
- SK 107 847
- Ⓐ SK 102 860
- Ⓑ SK 094 872
- Ⓒ SK 087 869
- Ⓓ SK 083 869
- Ⓔ SK 079 865
- Ⓕ SK 081 862
- Ⓖ SK 096 855

**PUBLIC TRANSPORT**
Infrequent bus service to Barber Booth

**REFRESHMENTS** Picnic site at start; cafés and pubs at nearby Edale

**PUBLIC TOILETS** At nearby Edale

**ORDNANCE SURVEY MAPS**
Explorer OL1 (The Peak District – Dark Peak area)

Follow the onward lane from the car park to Upper Booth. Beyond the buildings, dip to a bridge and then leave through a small gate on the right. The path twists above the wooded clough of Crowden Brook, eventually leading to a plank bridge. Climb beyond to pass through a gate onto the open access land of the National Trust's High Peak estate Ⓐ.

The landscape abruptly assumes a wilder character of rough grass, bracken and heather. Although poor grazing even for hardy sheep, it offers a good habitat for some and an information board describes wildlife that you might come across.

> **?** *What species of owl haunts the moorland slopes?*

The path accompanies the stream towards the higher valley, clambering over rocks and occasionally switching banks for an easier passage. The valley steadily closes in and, higher up, the looming crag of Crowden Tower dominates the head.

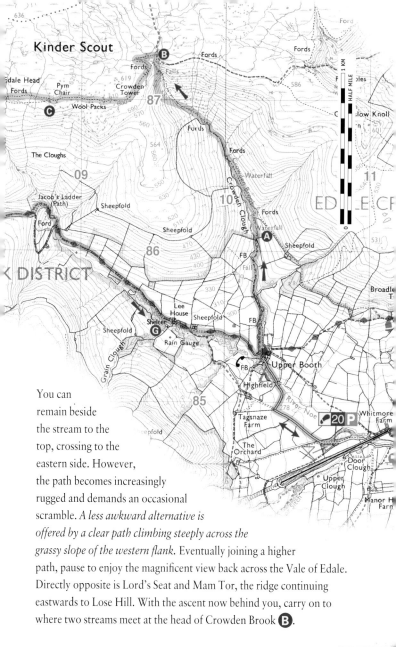

You can remain beside the stream to the top, crossing to the eastern side. However, the path becomes increasingly rugged and demands an occasional scramble. *A less awkward alternative is offered by a clear path climbing steeply across the grassy slope of the western flank.* Eventually joining a higher path, pause to enjoy the magnificent view back across the Vale of Edale. Directly opposite is Lord's Seat and Mam Tor, the ridge continuing eastwards to Lose Hill. With the ascent now behind you, carry on to where two streams meet at the head of Crowden Brook **B**.

*Looking up Crowden Clough to Crowden Tower*

A clear path climbs left above Crowden Tower before undulating onwards at the edge of the Kinder plateau. Often fragmenting, it picks its way through the peat and around the weird and wonderfully weathered boulders of the Wool Packs. Nature's unconscious artistry has produced many striking forms, some appearing anthropomorphic and others suggestive more of inanimate forms. They have inspired the work of many photographers and sculptors, including Henry Moore.

Farther on, prominent among the rocks is an outcrop known as Pym Chair **C** and later, the much larger, isolated formation of Noe Stool **D**. Here, the easiest path passes to the left of the rocky clump.

**Kinder** is a vast expanse of rolling peat hags and deep groughs. Bounded by abruptly steep, grassy rakes or precipitous, rocky edges, nowhere offers a line of easy ascent. Although the high point of 2,086 feet (636m) lies little over ¼ mile (400m) north of Pym Chair, with no obvious path, its attainment can be a challenge. *The going is rough and it is easy to become disoriented, particularly in poor weather. Unless you are experienced, the summit point is therefore best left to its windswept solitude.*

Beyond Noe Stool, the path has been improved and, curving south-west, begins to lose height. The Pennine Way subsequently joins from the right at a large cairn **E**. Continue down to a second junction and keep left on a flagged path, which curves down more steeply below Swine's Back to meet a stone track **F**.

Carry on steadily downhill, shortly coming to a fork beside a built cairn at the head of Jacob's Ladder. Either path will do, that to the right being somewhat longer but less steep, both leading to a narrow packhorse bridge spanning the River Noe.

Many steep routes are called Jacob's Ladder, referring to **Jacob's dream** described in Genesis, in which he saw a ladder between earth and heaven. The one here is fittingly named, for it was indeed cut by Jacob, not the Biblical patriarch of course, but Jacob Marshall who farmed the upper valley during the 17th century. It takes an ancient packhorse route from the Vale of Edale over to Hayfield. The bridge is probably even older. During medieval times packhorse teams were the haulage contractors of the day, and although barely 27 inches wide, the low walls of the bridge allowed easy passage.

Beyond a gate the track runs more easily through the widening valley to Lee Farm **G**. One of the barns has been restored as an information centre and inside, illustrated panels describe the area's natural and manmade histories.

Continue with the track to Upper Booth, there meeting your outward route to cross Crowden Brook. Follow the lane the ½ mile (800m) back to the car park. ■

*At the top of Jacob's Ladder*

# Further Information

## Safety on the Hills

The hills, mountains and moorlands of Britain, though of modest height compared with those in many other countries, need to be treated with respect. Friendly and inviting in good weather, they can quickly be transformed into wet, misty, windswept and potentially dangerous areas of wilderness in bad weather. Even on an outwardly fine and settled summer day, conditions can rapidly deteriorate. In winter, of course, the weather can be even more erratic and the hours of daylight are much shorter.

Therefore it is advisable to always take both warm and waterproof clothing, sufficient nourishing food, a hot drink, first-aid kit, torch and whistle. Wear suitable footwear, such as strong walking boots or shoes that give a good grip over rocky terrain and on slippery slopes. Try to obtain a local weather forecast and bear it in mind before you start. Do not be afraid to abandon your proposed route and return to your starting point in the event of a sudden and unexpected deterioration in the weather. Do not go alone. Allow enough time to finish the walk well before nightfall.

Most of the walks described in this book do not venture into remote wilderness areas and will be safe to do, given due care and respect, at any time of year in all but the most unreasonable weather. Indeed, a crisp, fine

Weir an River Lathkill

winter day often provides perfect walking conditions, with firm ground underfoot and a clarity that is not possible to achieve in the other seasons of the year. A few walks, however, are suitable only for reasonably fit and experienced hill walkers able to use a compass and should definitely not be tackled by anyone else during the winter months or in bad weather, especially high winds and mist. These are indicated in the general description that precedes each of the walks.

## Global Positioning System (GPS)

**What is GPS?**

Global Positioning System, or GPS for short, is a fully-functional navigation system that uses a network of satellites to calculate positions, which are then transmitted to hand-held receivers. By measuring the time it takes a signal to reach the receiver, the distance from the satellite can be estimated. Repeat this with several satellites and the receiver can then triangulate its position, in effect telling the receiver exactly where you are, in any weather, day or night, anywhere on Earth.

GPS co-ordinates, in the form of waypoint grid references, are used in *Pathfinder*® guidebooks, and many readers find the positional accuracy

GPS affords a reassurance, although its greatest benefit comes when you are walking in remote, open countryside or through forests.

GPS has become a vital global utility, indispensable for modern navigation on land, sea and air around the world, as well as an important tool for map-making and land surveying.

**Follow the Country Code**
- Be safe – plan ahead and follow any signs
- Leave gates and property as you find them
- Protect plants and animals, and take your litter home
- Keep dogs under close control
- Consider other people

(Natural England)

Langsett valvehouse

## Useful Organisations

**Campaign to Protect
Rural England**
5-11 Lavington Street,
London, SE1 0NZ
Tel. 020 7981 2800
www.cpre.org.uk

**Camping and Caravanning Club**
Greenfields House,
Westwood Way,
Coventry CV4 8JH
Site bookings Tel. 024 7647 5426
www.campingandcaravanningclub.co.uk

**Campaign for National Parks**
5-11 Lavington Street,
London, SE1 0NZ
Tel. 020 7981 0890
www.cnp.org.uk

**English Heritage**
The Engine House,
Fire Fly Avenue,
Swindon, SN2 2EH
Tel. 0370 333 1181
www.english-heritage.org.uk

**Forestry England**
Central England
Regional Office
Tel. 0300 067 4340
www.forestryengland.uk

**Friends of the Peak District**
37 Stafford Road, Sheffield,
S2 2SF
Tel. 0114 279 2655
www.friendsofthepeak.org.uk

**National Trust**
Membership and general enquiries
Tel. 0344 800 1895
www.nationaltrust.org.uk
*Hardwick Consultancy Office*
The Croft, Doe Lea,
Chesterfield, S44 5QJ
Tel. 01246 599430

**Natural England**
*Nottingham regional office,*
Apex Court, City Link,
Nottingham NG2 4LA
Tel. 0300 060 1111
www.gov.uk/government/
organisations/natural-england

**Ordnance Survey**
Tel. 03456 05 05 05
www.ordnancesurvey.co.uk

**Peak and Northern
Footpaths Society**
Taylor House, 23 Turncroft Lane,
Offerton, Stockport SK1 4AB
Tel. 0161 480 3565
www.peakandnorthern.org.uk

**Peak District National Park**
Aldern House, Baslow Road,
Bakewell, Derbyshire DE45 1AE
Tel. 01629 816200
www.peakdistrict.gov.uk

*Peak District Visitor Centres*
**Bakewell**
Old Market Hall,
Bridge Street, Bakewell,
Derbyshire
DE45 1DS
Tel. 01629 816558
**Castleton**
Buxton Road, Castleton, Hope
Valley S33 8WN
Tel. 01629 816572
**The Moorland Centre, Edale**
Fieldhead, Edale, Hope Valley
S33 7ZA
Tel. 01443 670207
**Upper Derwent**
Fairholmes, Bamford, Hope Valley
S33 0AQ
Tel. 01433 650953

**Ramblers**
2nd Floor, Camelford House,
87-90 Albert Embankment,
London SE1 7TW
Tel. 020 7339 8500
www.ramblers.org.uk

**Visit Peak District & Derbyshire**
Crescent View, Hall Bank,
Buxton, Derbyshire
SK17 6EN
Tel. 0845 833 0970
www.visitpeakdistrict.com

**Tourist Information Centres:**
Ashbourne: 01335 343666
Bakewell: 01629 816558
Buxton: 01298 25106
Castleton: 01629 816572
Leek: 01538 483741
Manifold Valley: 01538 483741
Matlock: 01629 583388
Saddleworth: 01457 870336
The Moorland Centre: 01433
670207
Upper Derwent Valley: 01433
650953

**Youth Hostels Association**
Trevelyan House,
Dimple Road, Matlock,
Derbyshire
DE4 3YH
Tel. 01629 592700
www.yha.org.uk

Kinder Scout

*Ordnance Survey maps of the Peak District*

**Explorer maps:**      OL1 (The Peak District – Dark Peak area)

OL24 (The Peak District – White Peak area)

*Answers to Questions:*

Walk 1:     Tip.

Walk 2:     It is 17 miles to Sheffield.

Walk 3:     Martin Davies.

Walk 4:     The King of Tonga in 1981.

Walk 5:     The Druid Inn.

Walk 6:     YHA for Youth Hostels Association.

Walk 7:     An information board lists Hands Well, Hall Well, Yew Tree
Well, Town Well, Coffin Well and Children's Well.

Walk 8:      May 24,1989.

| | |
|---|---|
| **Walk 9:** | By a cattle-grid. |
| **Walk 10:** | An information board gives the date 1863. |
| **Walk 11:** | SE 197 000. |
| **Walk 12:** | Red. |
| **Walk 13:** | Giant red deer and bear, according to the information board by the footbridge. |
| **Walk 14:** | Six years, according to an information board beside the Longdendale Trail. |
| **Walk 15:** | Victory, Defiant and Royal Soverin [sic]. |
| **Walk 16:** | Whinstone Lee Fields. |
| **Walk 17:** | The topograph indicates it is south of east, Middle Moor across which you walked is due east. |
| **Walk 18:** | Backhillgate, Windgather and Overton Hall. |
| **Walk 19:** | 1994. |
| **Walk 20:** | Short-eared owl. |

**Ordnance Survey**

## For more information visit

**www.pathfinderwalks.co.uk**
**tel: 01225 584 950**
**email: info@pathfinderwalks.co.uk**
**Twitter: @PathfinderWalks**
**Facebook: www.facebook.com/pathfinderwalks**